S0-APM-049

Teaching with the Wind

Spirituality in
Canadian Education

Michael Dallaire

Foreword by John P. Miller

UNIVERSITY PRESS OF AMERICA,® INC.
Lanham · Boulder · New York · Toronto · Plymouth, UK

Copyright © 2011 by
University Press of America,® Inc.
4501 Forbes Boulevard
Suite 200
Lanham, Maryland 20706
UPA Acquisitions Department (301) 459-3366

Estover Road
Plymouth PL6 7PY
United Kingdom

All rights reserved
Printed in the United States of America
British Library Cataloging in Publication Information Available

Library of Congress Control Number: 2011926285
ISBN: 978-0-7618-5553-8 (paperback : alk. paper)
eISBN: 978-0-7618-5554-5

∞™ The paper used in this publication meets the minimum
requirements of American National Standard for Information
Sciences—Permanence of Paper for Printed Library Materials,
ANSI Z39.48-1992

for Erin

Our work is to sow. Another generation will be reaping the harvest.

Dorothy Day, 1897–1980

Contents

Foreword

Education today at almost all levels focuses on the intellect, or put more bluntly, the emphasis is on teaching a *brain on a stick*. Those who find this view of learning too limiting have turned to holistic education and spirituality in education for a more inclusive vision of what should happen in our schools and universities. The field of spirituality in education has grown over the past decade with many new books published and conferences being held. Michael Dallaire's book is a significant addition to this field.

In books about spirituality the tone of writing is as important as the substance, and the tone here is pitch perfect. There is a contemplative quality to Dallaire's writing that resonated with me; at times the writing has a poetic quality. For example, consider the last lines of the book:

> To be a spiritual educator is ultimately not to provide all the answers but to help students to ask the correct questions and to set them upon the soul's path. The most crucial questions in life are those of the soul and so teaching, as the art of turning the soul to the world, needs to be learning to live a life for others with deeper questions always held within our vision. When the heart and the classroom are opened up to such searching, there is room for the wind to blow, fluid and unencumbered. This is what it means to teach with the wind.

This book explores the concept of the Canadian soul and nature (e.g. the wind) is one of the key facets of that soul. Other aspects described by the author are inclusiveness, justice, compassion, and compromise. Dallaire not only explores the positive aspects of these dimensions of the Canadian soul but also the shadow side of each dimension. This sense of balance can be found throughout the book. Dallaire argues that spirituality is the middle ground between the secular and the religious and it is in this space that we can renew education.

This book is directed to Canadians but there is much in this book that will appeal to other educators as well, particularly the suggestions for teaching. The author offers practical guidance to teachers to implement his vision in classrooms so that the soul of the student is nurtured. He suggests a path of presence, discernment, engagement and reflection. This path is explained with concrete examples so that educators can get a real sense of how this approach can work in the school curriculum. However, Dallaire's vision is an engaged spirituality that is not limited to the classroom. The writing includes examples from his own experience such as having students work at centers for the homeless or lobbying governments to enact progressive environmental legislation. These activities help develop what Dallaire calls a civic spirituality.

The author calls on teachers to engage in their own spiritual practices so that their teaching comes not just from the head but the soul. Again many examples of how teachers can do this, such as mindful walking, are presented. It is clear the author himself has engaged in a lifetime of spiritual practice so that writing reflects an authentic spiritual presence. I am grateful that Michael Dallaire has shared his work and sensibilities with us in this book and I hope educators seriously explore this vision in their lives and work.

John P. Miller,
Professor at The Ontario Institute for
Studies in Education at the University of Toronto

Acknowledgments

I am indebted to many individuals who have journeyed with me through-out this project. My thanks go out to Marilyn Yee, Maureen Fowler, and Catherine Kilbride who read early drafts and provided thoughtful critiques based upon their classroom practice. Thank you also to Tina Klein who edited the work and kindly polished the text from its rough stage to its current form. The responsibility for any blemishes in text or thought remains with me as author. I am grateful to the Center for Contemplative Mind in Society for permission to reproduce its *Tree of Contemplative Practices*, which provides an insightful visual aid for the issues discussed. Publication of this work was assisted with a grant received from Simon Fraser University and the Canadian Academy of Independent Scholars for which I am thankful.

My gratitude extends to the many teachers and students who over the years have given me their trust as we have explored the way of engaged spirituality within education. Your openness has been important for the work of spiritual animation in the school communities I've been honored to serve. To the administrators I've worked with over the years who have supported the work of spiritual education, I extend my gratitude as well. Moreover, I extend my thanks to those chaplain collaborators who have journeyed with me as we sought to break open a new path in the midst of the old. In the words of Stephen Biko, *pick up the spear where it has fallen.*

To John Affleck, who over the years offered me the gifts of listening and kindness, I am beholden. To Parker Palmer, who encouraged me to pick up my pen and to Jack Miller who encouraged me to continue when I was discouraged and ready to put it down, I express my heartfelt gratitude.

To my family and friends, I owe a litany of thanks for your support and encouragement as I explored this path. To the many kindred spirits I've met along the way, I express my appreciation for your echoes. To Erin Fowler, my life companion, I owe my deepest love and gratitude for without your patience, understanding, and support this work would not have come to fruition.

Introduction:
The *More* of Teaching

"And after the fire there came the sound of a gentle breeze."

1 Kings 19:13

When the terrorists attacked the United States on September 11, 2001, the Western world shuddered as we received a violent attack so uncharacteristic for our times, yet, too familiar for many people throughout our world. Understandably, we reacted in shock and disbelief at the horrific evil of the attacks as we watched the courageous acts of rescue workers, and communed with others to try to understand the event. The depth of the tragedy of that day unwittingly opened, albeit for a brief moment of time, a window of choice as to how to respond to such evil. We could choose to react in anger and fight back with military power to overthrow the *enemy*. Or we could choose to contain the violence by restraining the perpetrators while seeking to address the root causes that led to this violence. The leaders of the most powerful countries in the world choose the military response thereby escalating the violence rather than the path of containment and diplomacy aimed at curtailing violence. We now live in a time of continual *war on terror* with all its personal, social, and political consequences.

I was serving as chaplain in an inner city high school when the terrorists struck. This school had many students from around the world, some of who were escaping violence, war, and oppression in their homeland. The scale of the violence of September 11th impacted upon many of these students in particular ways, disturbing their fragile sense of self that often masquerades as invincibility. Like other schools, we offered prayers over the PA for the victims of the attacks and prayed for peace and justice. We lit candles and signed banners to be sent to the families of the victims. Like others, I struggled to come to terms with the previously unimaginable acts of terror. Most certainly, the death and destruction wrought by these acts only a few hours drive from Ottawa impacted heavily upon the consciousness of students and staff.

Therefore, when it was announced that there would be a public memorial on Parliament Hill to honour those who had been killed, I encouraged any staff and students who were able and willing to go to attend. I remember two young ladies, grade eleven students, who attended the memorial and who came to me afterwards to talk about it. They spoke of the huge number of people in attendance. They spoke of how good it felt to be there, to be able to stand with others, to be able to at least do something to express their shock, disbelief, and grief. They described how quiet it was on the Hill during the three minutes of silence that were offered in remembrance of the dead. The experience of thousands standing in silence appeared to them to be a fit and memorable way to remember the dead. These young women were moved by this memorial service and it assisted in their struggle to integrate the reality of such violence.

Within days of this memorial service I heard from several others who had been there and read in the local newspapers that there had been no references to God during the memorial. In respect for the diverse ethnic and religious fabric of contemporary Canada the organizers of the event obviously opted to omit any explicit or exclusive images of the divine. Many people were upset by this decision and saw the omission as a rejection of the Judeo-Christian God foundations of Canada. They interpreted this omission as evidence of the godlessness of our nation, and dismissed such omission as symptomatic of growing secularism in Canada. Implicit in such an interpretation is a judgment of the moral fabric of Canada, which in the eyes of these beholders, is more inclined to evil than to goodness. Such views persist and are unfortunately growing in Canada.

However, another way to look at this ceremony on Parliament Hill would have been to recognize that the service was a fitting civil liturgy that respected the multi-faith reality of Canada within a secular democracy. That being the case, the three minutes of silence and the absence of exclusive images of God, which were key components of the service, were not necessarily the rejection of God, but rather a way of giving voice to an inclusive and deeper expression of the mystical *more* that humans seek and from which we live. Silence may truly be the only appropriate way to commend the victims of the violence of the September 11th attack to the *more*. Silence is the primordial spiritual response of the human, the foundation of all spiritual speech and all mystical experience. It forms the ground for our knowing and longing for the *more* in our life, the *more* being that which calls us forth into life and which we seek at the depths of our hearts.[1] The role of silence in the spiritual life has a long tradition. In Judeo-Christian scripture, Elijah finds God in the gentle breeze, at the intersection of silence and the movements of nature. Christian and Buddhist practitioners throughout history have practiced the art of silence as a door to the mystical. In this light, silence and the absence of divine images can be understood as two of the necessary conditions for the possibility of giving voice to a civic spirituality in the midst of Canada's growing secular and multi-faith constituency.

This book is for teachers who serve this growing secular and multi-faith Canada. It is for teachers who teach in our post-911 world, a world where the secular and the religious, the spiritual and the mystical flow together. It is for teachers who seek tools to address the wounds of the soul that sometimes enter the classroom through the stories of their students or through world events over which they have no control but to which they must connect their teaching. It is for teachers who are seeking the ways and means to connect their teaching with a spirituality that comes alive for their students in the present moment. It is for teachers who keep their fingers on the pulse of the spiritual force that draws our attention despite the clanging of religious and secular fundamentalists of all stripes.

This book is for teachers who seek, beyond the tumultuous demands of the classroom, to see and feel the gentle breeze in life. It is for teachers who sense that there is something more to the life they lead and the life they are holding out for their students, a *more* which goes beyond that which is apparent and given. It is for teachers who sense this *more* in the universe on clear, bright cloudless nights when the stars overhead still draw out the wonder and awe of childhood. It is for teachers who seek the *more* in their inner universe where poetry and dreams are the guides and messengers of wisdom. It is for teachers who rise to the challenge to teach each time they see this *more* in the eyes of the students who enter the sanctuary of their classrooms. It is for teachers who, despite the challenges facing humanity today, sense the *more* of hope dawning on the horizon of our times. This *more* is the dimension of the spiritual, the soul, the ineffable and the mysterious, which draws the human heart towards awe and towards action.

From a conviction that there is a network of kindred spirits that stretches from coast to coast to coast, this book addresses the core concern of how to include an education for the *more* within the classrooms across our vast land. This network of kindred spirits is a community of public intellectuals[2] entrusted with the honorable task of forming the next generation of Canadians for participatory national citizenship. It is a community of front-line mentors who are mandated to pass on an appreciation for certain enduring skills, values, and attitudes that will help people to grow into the fullness of life within the opportunities that abound in Canada. Further, this book it is intended for teachers who know that the social, political, and spiritual dimensions of life cannot be barred from schooling and so must be intelligently and wisely integrated into the formation of the young. Finally, it is written for those educators who experience their profession as a summons to and from the *more* for within this call is found their vocation.

The intent of this work is to contribute to the public and professional discourse concerning the contentious issue of spirituality in Canadian education. I hope that some of the tools that are offered here to pursue this discourse can advance the public and professional discussion of spirituality in Canada's schools. Including this discussion within the teaching profession in Canada and within the halls of educational decision-makers will, hopefully, help to bring attention to the field of spiritual education that to date has been unfortunately, intentionally or unintentionally, omitted and overlooked.

Canadian educators work within a secular age in which the religious worldviews, while enduring and present, no longer hold primacy in terms of the organization of civil society. Our secular age does not necessarily dismiss the spiritual quest outright. It simply seeks to find new ways to pursue this quest as Charles Taylor in *A Secular Age* has so masterfully discussed.[3] The challenge of the secular mindset has begun to make inroads in some religious circles. In such circles secularist humanists are seen less and less as enemies and more and more as cooperators in a new time or even as offspring born from a religious family.[4] The ideas offered within these pages represent an attempt to work within the contours of secularity in a way that retains the best of religious approaches to spiritual education and encourages a dialogue between secular humanists open to the *more* and religious followers open to the *more* as experienced within Canadian history and culture.

We teach within an age in which our philosophical landscape is heavily influenced by postmodernism. Postmodernism is not a philosophy itself but rather a trend within philosophy. Philosophy influences our daily life in subtle and sometimes not so subtle ways for it gives direction to our systems of thought and our institutions. Within this postmodern trend there are those who promote pre-modern and modern philosophies of legitimization and postmodern philosophies of deconstruction and reconstruction.

We see the influence of pre-modern and modern philosophies when we embrace pedagogies that seek to legitimate a given worldview. Such pedagogies tend to be conservative and supportive of the status quo. They depend upon foundational stories and principled approaches to resolving ethical and moral dilemmas. Authority, whether located in persons, laws, or institutions, is respected and the value of obedience to authority is considered constitutive of personhood. Pre-modern and modern pedagogies always bring the questions and search of the individual back to the authority of the community rooted in either a text or a philosophical tradition. Legitimization as pedagogy is adverse to change, particularly radical change, change that goes to the root of all things. Much of contemporary Canadian educational practice is embedded in such pre-modern and modern approaches to learning. Initiatives that challenge the authority of core beliefs, hierarchies of power, and vested economic interests are given little leeway.

The postmodern pedagogies of deconstruction operate under a different set of philosophical assumptions. They promote a mistrust of the grand, foundational stories of culture, stories often located within religious or philosophical texts; ethical relativism and nihilism; a suspicion of authority; a valuing of difference at the expense of the common; a prizing of the personal autonomy in all matters; a vaulting of materialism over any sense of the transcendent; and a conviction that the pursuit of universals is an impossible dream given the complexities of cultures and diversity of meaning systems. The deconstructive impulse is very much alive within our public discourse and has contributed much to our society, especially in bringing the needs of marginalized voices to the attention of power brokers. Yet, the deconstructive approach, with its endless critique seldom offers realistic alternatives, which often leads to a chronic inability to creatively and responsibly meet the challenges of our times.

Postmodern reconstructive pedagogies, however, uphold the recovery of the wisdom to be found in grand narratives; the grounding of rights and authority within creative and holistic community; the existence of unifying elements across diversity; the pursuit of authenticity and integrity coextensive with systems; creative holism as a paradigm for the future; and a grounding in an ecological-mystical consciousness.[5] These reconstructive pedagogies are essentially pedagogies of hope rather than mistrust or resistance. The reflections offered in this book concerning spirituality in Canadian education are gathered around a pedagogy of hope in that they seek to recover the best of Western philosophical, religious and spiritual traditions and allow them to be reconstituted in light of today's secular Canadian society. They offer a progressive approach to developing a pedagogy for civic spirituality responsive to the needs of Canadians today.

Bringing the best of our religious traditions to bear upon our contemporary secular and pluralistic society requires embracing a method that encourages dialogue across different worldviews and traditions. Here, I am indebted to the work of Raimundo Panikkar who has been a leader in inter-religious and intercultural dialogue. In particular I find his appreciation of essence to be enlightening. Writing from his Christian roots Panikkar argues that we are witnessing today the dawn of Christianness, which is a stance in which the experience of Christ as the centering symbol of one's life is considered paramount. Christianness is the historical development of the Christian life beyond Christendom (a civilization organized along Christian principles) and Christianity (a religion). It is a mystical orientation that opens one to the *other*, to the world, and to the real in which one lives.[6] The stance of Christianness is one that moves from the essence of Christian experience outward to the *other* with whom one shares existence. In coming to own what one shares in common with the *other* we find a path across the boundaries of thought and knowledge, which more often creates strangers rather than citizens.

Panikkar has provided a way in which different religions can engage in dialogue together. Taken further, he has provided a stance in which religious adherents and secular humanists might dialogue and come to mutual understanding and shared action. Thus, we can conceivably have persons informed by different religions or even no religion discoursing about issues of common concern regardless of their differing horizons of meaning. The focus of such discourse would be on the search for truth of experience mediated by these different worldviews and by the truth that is emerging where these worldviews collide, collude, and commingle.

It is with this wide appreciation of each other that I invite the reader to enter into this exploration of spiritual education in Canada today. We are all invested in certain horizons of meaning that shape how we understand and know reality. My Christian horizon informs me but does not necessarily limit me for I am open to the *more* wherever it may be found. Some are perhaps informed by their secular humanist horizons. Others are informed by their Jewish, Muslim or Buddhist horizons. Some are informed by their aboriginal horizons. In these pages, I hope to develop a framework in which we can all dialogue about the shared appreciation for the *more* that we seek to live and express within our common experience of being Canadian. Such an approach need not diminish or discount the specific contribution of each horizon of meaning but rather provide room for it to be amplified and refined in terms of the challenges we all face.

As we proceed we need to appreciate not only how different approaches to the spiritual life are lived and practiced within Canadian education. We also need to reclaim our historical consciousness. A lamentable development, which has settled, unintentionally I believe, within our present educational practice is a forgetfulness of our history. This is due to the fact that history as a compulsory subject has been given reduced curricular time and attention in recent years. It is also because Canadian history has been subjected to pedagogies of deconstruction so that now we are suspect of any person or bodies that claim to teach history. Of course no history is unbiased but to choose not teach history amounts to professional negligence. What is needed is a recovery of Canadian history complete with critique and story so that the emerging generation is knowledgeable of the many different stories that inform our national consciousness. To fail to do so is to fail in our mandate to prepare students for informed citizenship. Moreover, it is to fail to provide the young with the grounding for the future, for if we forget and sanitize our past we have little, other than the present, upon which to build the future. This concern for the recovery of historical consciousness will be woven throughout these reflections.

My own roots can be traced to the arrival of my father's ancestors in Canada in 1658 when they settled on the eastern side of Isle D'Orleans on the St. Lawrence River. Immigrants from the French province of Brittany, they came to Canada, like most immigrants, to start a new life, one that held out possibilities they did not have in their homeland. My mother's ancestors came from France and Ireland, with the Kehoe's emigrating from Ireland in 1832, settling on a 100–acre farm just outside Navan, Ontario where they raised twelve children. My familial roots run long and deep within the Canadian context and help to shape my reflections here.

Born in Ottawa, I have been fortunate enough to live in various parts of Canada throughout my life. After a brief sojourn in France from ages two to five, I grew up mostly in southern Ontario. After graduating from high school and finishing my undergraduate degree at Queen's University I joined a religious order. During my twenties, as a member of that religious order, I lived in Ottawa, Edmonton, Happy Valley (Labrador), and even spent a brief time in Kugaaruk (Nunavut). After leaving religious life I continued my sojourning living at different times in Owen Sound (Ontario), Montreal, Ottawa, and, now, Vancouver. Having lived in various towns and cities across this country has helped me to appreciate the regional diversity that shapes our national consciousness. It has also deepened my appreciation for Canada. I have worked in these various locations as a teacher and a chaplain. I served for three years as an ecumenical community chaplain in social housing projects in Ottawa and followed this service with over twenty years as a high school chaplain. During these years I have grown in my appreciation for the various ways in which spirituality informs our lives and impacts upon our institutions. My travels and my experience, of course, have given shape to the reflections that follow, reflections, which I hope, will simply enliven the public discourse about why and how we educate within Canada today.

In the pages to follow I will explain the reasons why I hold that a civic spiritual education is important for us to pursue today. I will follow this with an argument in support of spirituality as a way of knowing, one that needs to be brought under the umbrella of Canadian education. I will present the notion of a Canadian national soul and point to how this can be recognized in our history and in our contemporary experience. The traditional method of contemplation-in-action, reconstructed as engaged spirituality, will be offered as an appropriate method for civic spiritual education in Canada. Some of the pedagogical concerns for using this method within our schools will be offered, as will be some reflections on the formation of teachers for this spiritual path. Finally, a few observations concerning the areas of management and governance as these apply to bringing such a civic spirituality into our education practice will be offered. At times I will refer to my own experience and at times I will ask the reader to reflect upon his or her own experience of teaching.

Teaching is a work of the mind, the heart, and the soul. It requires not only knowledge and skills but also a heart that listens to the *more*. This *more* animates our deepest desires, our widest potentials, and our strongest capacities. There are many different ways in which Canadian educators move and respond to the promptings of the *more*, ways often expressed in both religious currents and secular currents. As teachers of the *more*, often seen in the gentle breezes of life, we can be spiritual guides for our students on how to see and live from this *more*. In the following pages, I chart a course towards educating for a civic Canadian spirituality that is responsive to the emerging multicultural and multi-faith constituency located within our secular democracy. Should the musings in these pages contribute to the discourse urgently needed concerning spirituality in Canadian education then my objective will have been achieved.

NOTES

1. For a more complete study of prayer as first or primary speech, see Ann and Barry Ulanov, *Primary Speech: A Psychology of Prayer* (Atlanta, Georgia: John Knox Press, 1982).

2. Henry A. Giroux, "Teachers, Public Life, and Curriculum Reform" in *The Peabody Journal of Education,* ed. Susan Atkisson, Vol. 69, Nov. 3, Spring 1994. pp. 35–47.

3. Charles Taylor, *A Secular Age* (Cambridge, MA: The Belknap Press of Harvard University Press, 2007).

4. For a recent example of this discourse, see Ronald Rolheiser, *Secularity and the Gospel: Being Missionaries to Our Children* (New York: The Crossroad Publishing Company, 2006).

5. Joe Holland, "Toward a Global Culture of Life: Cultural Challenges to Catholic Social Thought in the Postmodern Electronic-Ecological Era" in *Globalization and Catholic Social Thought: Present Crisis, Future Hope,* eds. John A. Coleman and William F. Ryan (Ottawa, Canada: Novalis, 2005), p. 123.

6. Raimundo Panikkar, "The Dawn of Christianness" in *Cross Currents: The Wisdom of the Heart & the Life of the Mind,* Vol. 50, Nos. 1–2, Spring/Summer 2000. pp. 185–195.

Chapter One

Canadian Education and Spirituality

"All rivers run to the sea, but the sea is never full."

Ecclesiastes

Although I was born in Ottawa I did not grow up there. My father was in the Canadian military and so we were posted in different locations while I grew up. Still, our family would frequent that city as often as we could because it was where our extended families lived, my mother and father both coming from Ottawa. Periodically my brothers and I would be given to the care of aunts and grandparents over a holiday period to relieve our parents of the load of caring for four young boys. My great aunt Madeleine would take me into her home and care for me. Having never married and having no children of her own she treated me like royalty. For a young boy who was used to sharing his parents' attention with his brothers, the special care that I received from her was delightful.

Several times while in her care she would take me to the high bluff behind the Library of Parliament in Ottawa. From there we would watch the river-boats push the log booms towards the E.B. Eddy plant on the shore of the Ottawa River that flows from west to east. Into this river flows the Gatineau River from Quebec and the Rideau River from Ontario. The waters from these tributaries feed the Ottawa River which itself flows into the mighty St. Lawrence that in turn flows out to the Atlantic. In the distance you can see the beautiful Gatineau Hills, which during autumn are often resplendent with color. From this place successive governments have sought to guide Canada under the mandate of peace, order, and good government and to build a nation. While the lofty goals of peace, order, and good government have primacy in our contemporary telling of Canadian political history, John Ralston Saul has made a credible case that the genesis of our nation was more accurately peace, fairness and good government.[1] The exchange of order for fairness, however, did not erase the Canadian disposition towards justice and compassion.

Over the years I have often returned to this spot because it is an inspiration to me. Watching the quiet running river helps me to keep perspective on my personal life and on the events of the world. Here I am reminded that life is a journey, that there is a certain grace and a certain energy that flows through the events I have experienced. When my life is going well and full of meaning, the beauty of this river symbolizes the gift of life itself. During times when my journey has been more difficult, I have taken solace in the knowledge that there is a river of life I am following and its current beckons me onward. In addition to my personal life, I am aware that Canadians as a people are on a journey and there is a gracious river of meaning that flows throughout our history helping to provide direction for our collective journey. This location, behind the Parliament Buildings, in a political space, is a naturally spiritual place. Such a spiritual place provides a context to help reflect upon personal experiences and collective experiences. It helps to situate one's spiritual journey within the longer, historical context of Canada. It is a sacred place to meditate upon the nature of the Canadian soul. There are many such natural spiritual places across Canada, places where one is invited to ponder the mysteries of the Canadian soul and one's participation in that soulfulness.

The designation of Ottawa as the nation's capital at the time of Confederation was a surprise to many people. The conventional thinking at that time was that Kingston, Toronto, Montreal, or Quebec would be given the honour. Ottawa, known then as Bytown, was simply a rugged logging town nestled on the Ottawa River with only a little commerce and lacking in cultural life. It was certainly more out of the way than the larger cities of the Upper and Lower Canadas. Contrary to popular mythology, Ottawa was chosen by Canada's democratically elected representatives not by a distant monarch who knew little about the geography and political complexities of this new country.[2] There was wisdom in the selection. Bytown stood at a place where the two distinct founding cultures met and were joined by a flowing river. The intersection of the Gatineau and Rideau Rivers at the Ottawa River was a natural intersection and centering place for those who would govern a new nation. It also had the advantage of being a fair distance from the border of the United States. It was a natural place from which to nurture a new nation.

Those who dreamed of forming a country that would stretch from sea to sea to sea were carried by certain convictions that helped to give shape to their political vision for what would eventually become Canada. We know that they were seekers of balance. Feeling caught between the politics of Western Europe and their revolutionary neighbours to the South, they sought a political framework between a monarchy and a republic. Fearful of the largess of the United States and their not so hidden agenda of Manifest Destiny to acquire all of North America, they sought to bind a wide geographical area into a political reality that would enable its citizens to withstand the pressures for cultural, economic, and political assimilation by the United States. This historical fear of the American Manifest Destiny continues to fuel the anti-American sentiment that often permeates our Canadian discourse.

The founders of Canada were aware of the bilingual and bicultural nature of the original provinces and therefore sought to draft a constitution that would allow for a biculturalism within one national identity. Perhaps the greatest oversight of the founders was their complete disrespect for our First Nations, an oversight that fed the cultural genocide that preceded and followed Confederation and which we are only now beginning to unravel. Hindsight is often a luxury for historians. One certainly has to wonder what Canada would be like today if the cultural insights of our First Nations had been brought into our national identity rather than rejected. Would we have grown with more of an aboriginal or Metis sense of national identity as John Ralston Saul as argued?[3]

Mindful of the great expanse of land, the Fathers of Confederation sought to divide up the responsibilities for governing the vast resources and opportunities that existed. Primarily rooted in different Judeo-Christian traditions, they also sought to create a political framework in which religions would be permitted to influence but not dictate the affairs of the state. They did not advocate a complete separation of church and state but rather promoted an understanding that the religious voice would not hold final political power. Such a foundational partnership between religion and state laid the foundations for what is now emerging in Canada, a secular and pluralist democracy that provides a safe place for religious and spiritual people to thrive.

The founders of our nation could not have foreseen how multicultural, religiously pluralistic, and secular Canada would eventually become. Rooted in a Judeo-Christian worldview where diversity was experienced mostly as denominational differences, with a minor narrative of difference between Christians and non-Christians, they could not have foreseen the emergence of a multi-faith Canadian population residing in a secular democracy. The emerging multi-faith face of Canada in the midst of secularity has been a tremendous benefit for our country but it has also presented challenges. One such challenge is the need for education about diverse religious paths and the many ways in which people of different religious worldviews can cooperate and interact so as to contribute to the soul of our nation. Moreover, there is the need to educate for a civic spirituality, a spirituality rooted in the best of secular and religious humanism and broad enough to leave room for the particularities of religious and secular spiritualities. Prior to Confederation, there were schools in Upper and Lower Canada which provided basic education to small groups of children. In the early to mid-1880's such schools operated mostly upon Christian principles but they differed somewhat from the American approach to education. Indeed, as Emberley and Newell have discussed in *Bankrupt Education: The Decline of Liberal Education in Canada*, Canadian education in the pre-Confederation years was far more influenced by a spiritual and communal vision of society than it was by the Enlightenment vision of universal norms and individualism that drove the American social vision.

> This is the idea that education should take students out of themselves on a journey of the soul, beyond the familiar world of our own time and place with our particular attachments as citizens, family members, and friends. Education should show us wider horizons, and enable us to entertain the limited validity of our own way of life, so that we can return to it equipped with a greater appreciation for its achievements but also with a critical standard for assessing its shortcomings and making improvements where possible and prudent. Liberal education is, in short, a journey from the particular to the universal and back again.[4]

Thus, at the time of Confederation there was an understanding that education involved a unity of the spiritual and the intellectual life and a connection between education and active citizenship participation. It reflected the Platonic understanding of education as a process of turning the soul of the student to the life of the world. This turning of the soul hinged upon self-knowledge and a sense of duty to promote the common good of society. It promoted the journey of the soul to the wider horizons of the *more* and a return to live that *more* in one's daily life. Thus, the soul of the student and the soul of the world were taken as constitutive of the educational enterprise from the very beginnings of our country. Such an education was to be offered in a non-sectarian but nonetheless Christian way.

The one person who was particularly influential in setting the philosophical direction for Canadian education was Egerton Ryerson. He advanced a communal understanding of education and believed that education should be practical, open to the religious but not indoctrinating, universally available, and equal.[5]

> Egerton Ryerson, the School Superintendent of Canada West, pushed for free, universal, and an academically progressive public school system in what had been Upper Canada (now Ontario). He believed such schools would promote loyalty to the Crown, solid citizenship, a sound curriculum, and a generic Christianity.[6]

Not all Canadians accepted this approach to education. Specific religious groups, most notably Roman Catholics, rejected this educational philosophy as too generic and dismissed it as Protestant indoctrination. They lobbied long and hard for permission to run their own schools based upon their own specific theological convictions. Eventually "all the educational rights held by religious minorities as the time of Confederation would be secured constitutionally" under Section 93 of the BNA Act.[7] This approach allowed Catholics, and other religious minorities, to establish, manage and control their own schools. One can appreciate, in light of the religious tensions operative during those days, the significance of Constitutional protection that was extended to Catholics allowing them to have their own schools in Ontario and Manitoba. Unfortunately, due to the colonizing mentality of the times, aboriginal schools were not included. Section 93 of the BNA Act would be the focal point for the growth or elimination of religious schools throughout Canada's history. It would also be the legal mechanism that would legitimize the inclusion of diverse minority voices within the larger project of education across Canada.

Despite the different theological orientations between the Ryersonian approach to education and the approach of religious minorities, they found common ground in the need to educate for a virtuous citizenry able to shoulder their responsibilities to promote the common good. More likely, they saw religion and spirituality as synonymous and did not distinguish between the two as we do in our day. Neither did they separate or eliminate the religious from the sphere of the state. No, religious worldviews were implied and presumed in the public imagination. It is important to remember, then, the impact which religion had upon Canadian education and to recognize that religion was a thread that ran through our culture. It should not surprise us today in our secular age that we continue to wrestle with the visions brought to expression through our education systems. While some may desire to eradicate religion from the Canadian classroom, to do so would be unfaithful to our beginnings. It would be especially unfaithful to attempt do so without at least seeking to formulate a means to address the deeper issues which religious education addresses, issues of the soul in the world. Hence, we need to find a way to explicitly bring spirituality into our Canadian schools.

Obviously, early Canadian educators were dealing with different problems than we do today in our era of globalization and technocracy. Yet, it is important to note that they were dealing with similar themes as we do today. How would they deal with regional diversity while promoting a national unity and identity? How would they avoid the worst of religious extremism, while maintaining respect for religious and cultural diversity? How would they educate for responsible citizenship across a vast territory that fostered isolation rather than connection? How would they maintain a distinct Canadian identity while living so close to the United States of America and so distant from the parent nations in Europe? The founders of Canada rose to the challenges of these questions by enunciating a view of Canada as a community of communities, where there would be a federal government to protect areas of common interest and provincial governments to protect regional interests. They came up with a political formula that has stood the test of time.

However, a weak link in the founding blueprint of our nation was the fact that education was designated a provincial jurisdiction rather than a federal one. So, with the absence of a federal leadership role and oversight, the onus fell upon the shoulders of the provinces to provide for the education of Canadians. Obviously, provincial ministries of education will favor educational theories and policies that build up the provincial character rather than the national one. Indeed, the lack of a distinct federal oversight of education has contributed to the fragility of a specific Canadian identity as Canada has grown.

The impact of the absence of a strong centering vision of education has been compounded over time by the emergence of a secular and pluralistic democracy. Indeed, as the eminent Canadian philosopher Charles Taylor has so eloquently argued in *A Secular Age*, the context for living out religious and spiritual questions today is not the same context for living them out in 1867. Canadians are part of a larger historical transition from a worldview where it was impossible to think of life without reference to religion to a worldview where it is entirely acceptable to do so. The emergence of the secular and pluralist world we currently live in took place over a period of several hundred years, a period during which the land we now call Canada was conquered by Europeans and established as a nation. The emergence and development of Canada has taken place during this time of transition. Without a strong federal oversight of education, it is easy to understand how the sentiments of the founders to provide education in a soulful manner were easily lost and forgotten. This loss of vision has been to our detriment for there is a soul to being Canadian and to forget this soulfulness is to lose touch with a necessary ground for engaging the issues of our time.

AN AXIAL AGE

Few teachers today would deny the fact that we are living during a time of enormous change. Driven by our technological and scientific achievements, we teach in a time of previously unimaginable discoveries and innovations. Moreover, the dawn of computer technology and the Internet era have brought the explosion of knowledge right into our classroom each day. Indeed, the growing availability of technological aids and the electronic media are changing the day-to-day practice of teaching and learning, thereby transforming the role of a teacher. While there are tremendous benefits in the explosion of knowledge driven by science and technology, if technology is pursued within education as if it had intrinsic value rather than instrumental value the possibility of manipulating the human person towards a limited worldview increases.

In this technological age we are inundated almost daily and immediately with the many different crises that swirl around our globe. There are many ecological crises often caused by our lack of communion with the natural world. There are also many wars rooted in, or exacerbated by, racial, religious, or political prejudices. The presence of overwhelming hunger, poverty and disease, particularly AIDS, often caused by neglect, greed, or ignorance stagger our imaginations. These realities have led some, like Canada's own public intellectual Jane Jacobs, to call ours a dark age[8] akin to the dark ages that preceded the Middle Ages. In addition to her comment, many have opined that, with the dawning of the computer age, we are caught up in transformation of civilization of the magnitude akin to the changes ushered in with the invention of the printing press. The cacophony of these global problems seems to cripple our ability to respond effectively. No matter how technologically advanced we become we seem unable to eliminate poverty and hunger, disease and illness, war and violence.

Culture can be imagined as a sea of ideas, values, and traditions that forms the container for our voyage through life. In this context, there is plenty of evidence to suggest that we are living in a time of turbulent seas, a time of great cultural change. Ours is an axial age when the foundations of cultures and civilizations are being shaken. During this time of change there are some countries enjoying relative tranquility where peace and prosperity are the predominate traits. Canada is one such place. Most people within our country are enjoying a standard of living greatly enhanced by advances in science and technology. We are the beneficiaries of modern advances in health care and inheritors of a hard won public health care system. We enjoy a longer life span, cultural diversity, increased wealth accumulation, and a respected reputation on the world scene. We are inheritors of a national history relatively free of military conflict on our own soil and are witnesses to the steady development of democracy and human rights within our borders. For a relatively young nation, we have much going for us and much for which we can be thankful. With our nation surrounded by three distinct oceans and contained by the longest border in the world, we are fortunate in so many ways. In the midst of the numerous storms of our times, Canada is a relatively calm place to be.

Yet, Canadians are not immune to the effects of the turbulence through which humanity is passing. We see the effects of environmental destruction in our own land. One need only fly over British Columbia to see the ravages of clear-cutting or over the oil fields and tar sands of Alberta to see the impact of oil extraction. One need simply to experience the closure of beaches in Ontario on a hot summer day or experience the precariousness of our drinking water to know the impact of pollution upon our life. On top of our ecological concerns, we see the growing gap between the rich and the poor in our country, the increasing economic pressures placed upon working families, and the spread of homelessness across our nation. Moreover, in our age of terrorism we have our own examples of those who would use violence to achieve their political ends. The FLQ bombings in Quebec in the 1960's and the Air India bombing are contemporary Canadian examples of violent political actions undertaken by our own citizens. We recognize that much of the violence throughout our world is rooted in religious and racial bigotry, and yet we are not immune to such bigotry. The persistence of an anti-immigrant sentiment in Quebec, which caused the establishment of the Consultation Commission on Accommodation Practices Related to Cultural Differences, points to the reality of racism and religious intolerance, which simmers just below the surface of much of Canadian society. Finally, the Internet has been put to much good use but is also being used for unsavory, illegal, and unethical behaviour. Canadians are not immune to the effects of online child pornography, online gambling addiction, identity theft, and a general sense of disengagement from civic life that is one of the downsides of pervasive Internet usage.

Our age, then, holds a mixture of tranquility and turbulence. The blending of these forces plays upon our consciousness daily, mostly through the telecommunication industry and the media. These windows to the world are almost always open unless we make a deliberate decision to close them. Such constant inundation has an effect upon our hearts. Unlike previous eras, when it could take days or even weeks to learn about a significant achievement or disaster, we often learn of such events as they are happening. The immediacy of such knowledge, without the buffering distance of time and space between event and witness, has created an informed consciousness for sure. However, it is a saturated consciousness where naïveté is low and paralysis is high, where knowledge is abundant but wisdom is scarce. Two consequences of this saturated consciousness are often inertia and apathy. Indeed, this consciousness can lead to a sense of hopelessness in the face of such overwhelming challenges. It can lead to a sense of being adrift without a compass in a sea of change.

Our ability to comprehend these realities is further compromised by the fact that we no longer have a unifying worldview to provide us with a common set of tools through which to negotiate, understand, and engage the issues we face. Such tools were often given by religion through rituals, doctrines, superstitions, and practices that sought to interface the divine and the human. We live in the postmodern era, one that denies the legitimacy of any grand narrative and begrudgingly acquiesces to a plurality of petite narratives as guides to life. Moreover, as Charles Taylor[9] has argued, the rise of our secular age has resulted in the diminishment of the religious in the public square and has also made what was once unthinkable, the credibility of unbelief, an acceptable worldview. We have today a mosaic of worldviews in which religious, agnostic, and atheistic worldviews coexist within an overarching state philosophy of secular democratic humanism reinforced by capitalism. One of the positive features of this secular age is an increased understanding between once seemingly incommensurable worldviews. We see this understanding taking place when people are brought into conversations with the *other* who is different from them. On a positive note these conversations are contributing to a more sophisticated and mature citizenry, better able to deal with diversity and complexity. On a negative note, such diversity contributes to a pressure that fragments any common framework and diffuses the collective energy required to solve the problems we face as Canadians and as global citizens.

Teachers, who stand and deliver at the intersection of knowledge and the thirst for knowledge, know firsthand the impact of living in a time of tremendous change. Such is the context in which those of us who are concerned with education work and it is the backdrop for those who parent the next generation of citizens. This context of stormy seas is the world's curriculum. It is what we so often refer to as the real world. Evidence of this real world curriculum lies not only in our media-saturated consciousness and the ever-increasing influence of immediate telecommunications upon our awareness, but also in the very real life stories of our students who come to us each and every day. The real world curriculum is in the minds of parents who engage the stormy seas of the world in their places of work and who return to their homes tasked with mediating hope, love and joy to their children. Many of the individual stories, which our students carry in their very beings, are connected to the world curriculum where the forces of good and evil, progress and decline are at play. It is in the midst of this sea of change that teachers and parents seek to pass on enduring values to the young, values that they hope will sustain them throughout the journey of life. In our time of historical change, many parents turn to our schools for assistance and wisdom on how to raise children capable of navigating well the unknown seas ahead. Many teachers, parents and students turn to the education systems across our land to provide some insight and knowledge to help prepare us for civic engagement. Granted, there are other sources of insight and knowledge, but surely our schools are one the major sources sanctioned by society.

The human person is a meaning-seeking creature. The search for and creation of meaning is located within our ability to reflect upon experience and through this reflective experience we acquire knowledge and, over time, wisdom. This capacity for reflection is aided through many different ways and means, which are often passed on to us via the community or culture we live in. This search for meaning is at its core a spiritual search.[10] The capacity for consciousness and the search for purpose and meaning point to spirituality as being part of what it means to be human. Spirituality is essential to our sense of being fully alive.

Spirituality is only slowly being publicly acknowledged in our secular age. The reasons for this are many. First, in our secular age spiritual concerns have often been relegated to the periphery as the domain of religious caretakers and most certainly omitted in the political arenas. In a time like ours, one that has diminished the impact of religious voices from the public sphere, the result has been a loss of spiritual insights as they apply to public and political life. Second, the plurality of religions makes it difficult to give voice to a unifying spiritual approach especially in the areas of social and ecological action. Indeed, in our postmodern secular age that upholds the cacophony of pluralism without unity it is difficult to talk about what we share in common, a discourse that is absolutely essential for spirituality. Thirdly, there is a poverty of language and symbols in the secular sphere to facilitate discourse about spirituality. Poets, singers, artists, and writers valiantly give expression to their experiences of the spiritual, the numinous and the ineffable, but such expressions are rarely encoded into our public institutions so as to facilitate the teaching and learning of these insights. The language, symbols, and stories required for expression are emerging, but a systematized approach for communicating these has yet to be accepted in such a way that would facilitate talk about civic spirituality. Finally, there are areas of our world where the spiritual, the social, and the political have been integrated. We find that these expressions have either been wrongfully discounted, as in the case of much of political theology in Europe and liberation theology in Latin America, or rightfully dismissed, as is the case with militant religious fundamentalism. There are numerous reasons why we have not yet been able to up the discourse on spirituality in the civic arena.

Still, there are emerging signs of change. More and more people are interested in spirituality, ethics, and living with purpose. We are witnessing a burgeoning of interest in these areas outside the religious sphere and in the public square. The growth of socially responsible investment organizations and ethics boards within institutions is evidence of this trend. The ecological movement is a good example of engaged spirituality, for what is the concern for ecology if not concern for what binds us together upon this good earth? In the area of health care, in particular, we are seeing the gradual inclusion of spirituality as a component to holistic health care. Finally, at the foundation of society, the family, we find parents who continue to seek ways to imbue their offspring with their traditions, values and spiritual outlook, which are particular to each family unit. Despite the challenges of educating for spirituality in our secular age there are many historical vectors that are in movement supporting such an education. This task of forming the next generation of citizens in spirituality is one that parents share with teachers who stand *in loci parentis*. Parents and teachers together are the directors of initial formation in the ways of the spirit.

In Canada, as with many other countries in the Western world, we have essentially two streams of education. One is secular and the other is religious. Within these two streams, we find schools across Canada operating with either full or partial public funding depending upon the differentiated funding formulae found across Canada. These two streams of education are legally protected in the Canadian constitution and are linked to the visions for education that were operative around the time of Confederation. Both streams have been influenced over the years by the change from a bicultural and Judeo-Christian nation to a multicultural, multireligious, and secular nation. Ultimately, the different ways in which these two streams engage the questions of spirituality are being challenged in themselves by the historical changes currently affecting Canadians. One should not be surprised to find that challenges to the legal and financial status of these different schools would be part of our contemporary political discourse. However, as I am seeking to articulate, one need not move uncritically towards changing the legal or funding arrangements that are present at the moment. Rather, as will become clearer, there is a need to provide governance that is in keeping with the changing nature of education that reflects the changes in our Canadian population.

CURRENTS OF THE SPIRIT

The prevailing philosophy of a secular worldview in the West is to uphold the autonomy of the individual through the use of reason. It is through the use of reason that the human person gives shape to the world and contributes to the development of human communities that in turn sustain the human person. The secular worldview is often liberal in that it stands upon the notion of society as a social contract, between rational, consenting persons wherein all is permitted as long as it doesn't impose upon the freedom and peace of others. In the secular world, democracy and human rights, primarily understood as individual rights, are hallmarks. Conspicuously absent from the secular public discourse is any talk of transcendent or otherworldly spiritualities especially if such talk undermines the value of wealth and prestige. If there is any talk of spirituality in the secular stream, it is of a spirituality that places human accomplishment at the center of the quest for meaning.

Our Canadian public school system is primarily guided by this secular philosophy. Our public schools do an excellent job in educating students regardless of economic, cultural, linguistic, racial, and religious differences. This education system promotes civic values of democracy, equality, freedom, and social justice, values of our common good and hallmarks of Canadian society. Moreover, many students in public schools are infused with a sense of citizenship and global solidarity through altruistic service and humanitarian projects.

The appeal of secular education for parents is that this education promises to prepare their children for the world of work while socializing them into the norms of the prevailing culture. Schools therefore help parents to raise their children to be happy and productive citizens. Despite some obvious limitations to public education, particularly underfunding and overcrowding, most parents feel that the education provided helps to bring their sons and daughters into the good of society. Such an education accepts society as it is, and seeks to mentor and prepare the young for adult participation in secular democracy.

However, secular education is not without its secular critics. Neil Postman in his famous book *The End of Education* wrote about how the gods of consumerism, technology, and ethnic separatism have failed to provide a sound foundation for public education for they cannot provide a unifying narrative that holds the inquisitive heart. Without going towards the direction of revealed and transcendent narratives of religion, Postman argues that we need to retrieve learning as a communal project and relocate the goal of education within the common good.[11] Education for civic spiritual engagement would complement the direction Postman proposes.

The religious stream of education is informed by a very different philosophy, not the least of which is an understanding of the person as being related to a divinity of some sort. It is more apt to speak of religious streams given the variety of religions, but for our purposes here we will speak of what is common to all streams. Often there is a core text, which is revered and considered normative for the worldview. A sense of community and belonging to a community is a constitutive component of religious worldviews as is the sense of service to others. Normally, there is a clear ethical code. One of the hallmarks of the religious stream is a transcendental spirituality, one that places the rewards for worldly engagement in an afterlife. There is an appreciation for immanence in the spiritual life, but this concern is often eclipsed by the otherworldly concerns particularly within the conservative forms of religion.

The appeal of the religious streams of education for parents is based on many factors. Since religious identity and cultural identity frequently reinforce each other, faith-based schools are often seen as a way of maintaining cultural identity, which makes them very attractive to new immigrants. They are also seen as places for inculcating a coherent moral vision different from the prevailing culture, a feature that many religious parents value. They can be perceived as providing a more comprehensive, more disciplined, and superior education to that offered through public education. Whether these perceptions stand up to objective scrutiny is a question for another time. Despite the challenges with secure sources of funding, these schools will continue to thrive and grow, partly due to immigration and the growing multi-faith nature of Canadian society, but also partly due to a declining parental confidence in the public education system's ability to offer a unified and coherent moral framework.

Sometimes we are able to witness places where the secular and religious streams of education overlap or co-exist. For example, within the teaching profession itself there are overlaps. Many teachers who work within faith-based schools are imbued with secular philosophy. Conversely, many teachers working in the public school system live from religious worldviews and seek to quietly witness to the values upheld within these worldviews through their daily lives. Thus, through the lives of individual teachers the two streams of thought intermingle. In fact, the dualism, which once allowed us to designate the religious and secular, has begun to break down, so much so that we see beginnings of the blending of both orientations, which provides a challenging yet ripe opportunity for spiritual education. Indeed, the time is ripe for a new humanist education that would be a gathering place for both religious and secular educators. The common denominator of such a new humanism would be the human person, as embodied soul, open to the *more* experienced and acquired through engagement in the social and common good. Such openness to the *more* provides one of the conditions for the possibility of a civic spirituality.

Generally, these two streams of education cooperate whenever possible. I am reminded of one Catholic school in southwestern Ontario that shared a building with a secular public school. The two different schools shared a common library, gymnasium, and cafeteria. The teaching staff, curricula, and management philosophies were what differentiated the two schools. Even where facilities are not shared, school administrators often coordinate their programs and share buses, sports facilities, and avoid simultaneous school dismissal.

There are many instances in which these two streams compete and fail to cooperate. In fact, there are sometimes ways in which they subtlety work to undermine the good of each other. For instance, when Canadian secular education is practiced in such a way that religious narratives are silenced, it does little more than indoctrinate students in the narrative of secular materialism.[12] This silencing does not serve the Canadian common good in the long term since religious narratives offer support, and critique, of the secular stream thereby strengthening it. The corrective function of religious narratives in fact contributes to the clarification and development of the secular narrative that informs our nationalism thereby ensuring a healthier and more vibrant society for all.[13] The other side of the debate is just as true too. When religious worldviews are critically and creatively challenged by secular insights what often results is the clarification and development of religious life and practice. Since people of religious convictions live within secular society, the fruits of the secular challenges ultimately make the religious presence within society stronger and clearer.

Ideally, there ought to be a healthy and mutually correcting dialectic between religious and secular streams of education within our nation, a dialectic that should ultimately strengthen our country. Unfortunately, this healthy exercise rarely takes place between the two streams of education. Too often, due to suspicion and misunderstanding, the public conversation between the secular and religious streams of engagement sinks to caricatures and bitter debates. Whenever religious sentiments intrude upon the secular stream of education, inevitably forces come into play to push the religious insights back into the private life or back into the religious enclave. Likewise, very often when secular insights intrude upon the religious stream of education, forces come into play to push the secular insights out of the religious realm and relegate them to the common space of secular society where they can be, presumably, ignored or at least marginalized from the religious group's consciousness. It appears then that the struggle between secularism and religion runs straight through the heart of the Canadian educational enterprise today just as it does through Canadian society itself.

Lois Sweet, in *God in the Classroom* (a well-researched book on religion in Canada's schools), documented the struggle between faith-based and public schools within Canada today. Towards the end of her work she acknowledged that, while including education about religions within Canada's public schools would be a worthy practice, there was no provincial jurisdiction willing to move in this direction.[14] Moreover, the recent Ontario Provincial election of 2007 demonstrated just how divisive is the issue of religion and education within our secular society. During that election, the decisive issue was whether or not to extend full funding to all faith based schools since such funding had already been granted to the Catholics schools in that province. It appears that there is not the political will to extend full funding to religiously based schools at present. Given this lack of will, we can expect the proliferation of faith-based schools, a potential widening of the present rifts between public and religious schools, and the continual disregard of the spiritual impulse within Canada's public education system.

Such a situation is regrettable. If many of the social and ecological problems we face are exacerbated by our lack of a spiritual depth in everyday life, then the refusal to support schools that include the spiritual dimension as part of their overall philosophy is shortsighted. In order to arrive at appropriate solutions to our social and political problems, we need to include the spiritual dimension of life. However, given the political and philosophical deadlock concerning the funding of religiously based schools across Canada, I think we need to widen and deepen our approach to education.

A NEW CURRENT FOR A NEW TIME

We need to move away from the irreconcilable differences between religious and secular streams of education and seek a new cooperative spiritual path. We need a new path that will run through both secular and religious schools and unite the good in both to deepen our action and attention to the social, political and ecological concerns of our times. In a sense, we need to channel our energies into a larger river, one that can provide the spiritual energy to be responsive to the challenges of our day. If we can cooperate in addressing the pressing issues that face us as a nation, issues that are often ecological and economical in nature, then we can hope that common actions will provide us with a common heart. Indications of this new way can be found in those who are researching and teaching about spirituality in education regardless of their system locations.[15]

Education for spirituality of course already takes place within many religious schools across Canada where great efforts are made to extend the practice of religion and spirituality across the entire school project. These efforts include the hiring of teachers, the curricula itself, the methods of discipline, and the allocation of budgets. These schools are able to reach within the depths of their traditions and to give voice to the spiritual path as envisioned by their particular religion. Such teachings often give preference to the transcendent over the immanent in spirituality, but they nonetheless do uphold the importance of the care of others and of the stranger.

Spiritual education is also taking place within secular, public schools. Indeed, there is a nascent movement to include contemplative practices, meditation, values and character education, and holistic education in the public schools. For example, in Vancouver public schools there is a movement to include attention to values, ethics, empathy, and civics. These are doors to spirituality for they point to the more to life beyond mere knowledge and skills. Elsewhere, Professor John P. Miller at the Ontario Institute for Studies in Education at the University of Toronto has been a pioneer in the field of holistic and spiritual education and is providing theoretical and curriculum guidance often with an appreciation for Buddhist practices. His work is a response to the growing desire to include spiritual education within Canada's secular education system.[16] In Quebec, we find the Ministry of Education promoting the provision of spiritual care animators in its non-confessional system of schooling.[17]

While spiritual education is still an emerging field, I think we can build upon this current practice within our Canadian education systems in such a way that it advances both the secular and religious streams of education. Spiritual education can provide a middle way that both religious and secular advocates can embrace, a way that incorporates the best of both the religious and the secular worldviews and avoids the pitfalls inherent in both. Such an approach would be rooted in the best of humanist tradition and provide a meeting point across religious and secular traditions. It would be an approach that would be in keeping with Panikkar's suggestion of promoting the essence of one's path. A spiritual education that is responsive to Canada's identity in an ever-growing pluralist and secular democratic state and that helps to form citizens better able to address the social and ecological problems we face would be an education worth promoting.

As an educator and a chaplain, I have long been concerned with how the social and political dimensions of life provide both the context and the container for the expression of personal spirituality. That is, our private and personal spirituality comes to its fullest expression in society and politics and is, at the same time, shaped by society, culture and politics. The mystical has social and political implications and the social and political dimensions of human life have mystical underpinnings. With this understanding we can see that the social and political dimensions of Canadian life are part of what can be called a Canadian soul. This Canadian soul forms a container for the development of individual spirituality and is essential to the formation of Canadian citizenship. If this Canadian soul can be highlighted it could provide a suitable framework for the legitimate education in spirituality in Canadian schools, both faith based and public.

The notion of a Canadian soul will appeal to both religious persons whose allegiance is to faith-based horizon of meanings while keeping a foot in the *secular* world and secular humanists whose allegiance is to the secular horizon of meaning while keeping their options open to the *more* in life. In truth, teachers abide in both streams of meaning to various degrees depending upon their own personal convictions and the specific locations, secular or faith-based, for their professional practice. In my view, the time is ripe to highlight education for humanist spirituality and to bring this into the mainstream of education, both public and faith-based, in Canada. Education in spirituality could help to offset both religious and secular indoctrination, counteract religious and secular fundamentalism and meet the growing need for an education in character and values for the next generation. Such a middle way would be very much in keeping with the historical Canadian experience with creative compromise. Ultimately, educating for a middle way would enhance our national identity and contribute to making Canada a desirable oasis of meaning in today's global village.

DEFINING SPIRITUALITY

The reader will, perhaps, agree with me thus far in the need to highlight the spiritual dimension within education in Canada. Now, two important and interrelated questions need to be asked. First, what is spirituality? Second, how do we educate for this dimension? The first question will be developed more extensively in chapter three while the second question will occupy the concerns of the fourth and fifth chapters. For now, let me offer a few preliminary outlines of an answer to these questions.

Clive Beck, a self-professed secular humanist, has argued for the inclusion of religion and spirituality in schools. He argues for what he calls a broad understanding of spirituality as including: awareness, breadth of outlook, a holistic outlook, integration, wonder, gratitude, hope, courage, energy, detachment, acceptance, love, and gentleness. Such a broad definition would be acceptable to both secular and religious educators, although he recognizes that some religious persons will not be satisfied with this definition because it omits the ineffable or otherworldly dimensions. Furthermore, he argues that spirituality must be concerned with both interiority and exteriority, that is, the inner disposition of the learner and the world in which the learner is living. Beck believes that it is necessary and important to include religion and spirituality in schooling and that this inclusion can be achieved in ways that avoid indoctrination. He even goes so far as to advocate for its inclusion in countries where religion and spirituality are excluded from schooling based on the notion of a complete separation of church and state.[18] I agree with Beck that we need to understand spirituality in a broad sense, and I agree with the characteristics of a spiritual person, which he puts forth. In my view, these observable characteristics are the result of following a spiritual path. What needs attention is how to teach a spiritual path in our schools.

I would like to propose a broad definition of spirituality as a lifestyle in which a person aligns himself or herself with the animating energy operative in the universe and manifest daily in the realities of concrete life. This notion of animating energy has traditionally been recognized by philosophers and theologians as the soul. Soul is present in the natural world, in the creative life of the human community, and in the heart of each individual who lives and breathes and shares his/her being with others. Spirituality, then, is about paying attention to the presence of the soul, the animating principle, in all of life. Spirituality is also concerned with becoming aware of the absence of soul when that too is the case. It is about living in congruence with the insights and demands of the soul that operates both in the world and in our deepest selves. This understanding of spirituality as attending to and living from the soul is one that would be acceptable to both secular and religious worldviews for the concept is found in both.[19]

There is a need to ground this general definition of spirituality of living congruently with and from the soul within a particular context, a specific historical moment, and a unique perspective. In effect, spirituality needs to be concrete and particular as well as abstract and universal. The best way to do this is to bring spirituality beyond the confines of the interiority to the exteriority of lifestyle and into the communal, the social, and the national realms of life. In a sense, we need to move towards embracing a civil spirituality, one that connects and inspires.

We are not without roots in this civil spirituality. The Canadian soul, while similar to other nations' civil spirituality, has characteristics that are particularly Canadian. This national soul is a particular manifestation of the world soul, mediated through the prism of Canadian history and culture. Our most obvious vocalists for this civil spirituality have been our poets and our visual and audio artists. Through their creations, we have been given glimpses of our national soul.

A national soul bridges the gap between the individual and the world soul. It moves from the local and the particular to the global and the universal. In this sense, it builds towards the universal through the recognition of local cultures and nation states. Building towards transversalism recognizes that the move towards the universal common good is achieved through the cooperation of the local and particular good found in local cultures. Thus, a concept of the national soul serves the need of our time to find language that expresses the largess of the *anima mundi* while respecting the diversity of its expression within different cultures and nations. As I hope will become clear throughout these pages, Canadian education needs to pay deliberate attention to the concerns of the national soul and to educate for this spiritually. Moving spiritual education to the front of the classroom, to the center of our board meetings, and to the core of our philosophy of education will require a recognition and re-affirmation of our national soul.

The second question concerns the question of method. How do we educate for spirituality, for such a Canadian soul? I would like to suggest that the time-honored path of contemplation-in-action, found in all world religions and within secular philosophy itself, is a credible way for spiritual education within the Canadian scene. The integral way of contemplation-in-action is a path that resonates with both secular and religious persons and it can have currency for use in all Canadian schools, faith based or secular public. When we direct our contemplative and active lives to the facilitation and nurturance of our national soul we have essentially a civic spirituality.

There are many who would dispute that we can come up with an acceptable and comprehensive definition of Canadian soul, let alone that we can agree upon an acceptable method for educating for such a Canadian soul within our formal education systems. Such reservations can be due to an ingrained suspicion of a coming up with a single notion of Canadian spirituality in a land of such regional, cultural, racial, and religious diversity. I do not want to dismiss these concerns, for there is some legitimacy in them. We do risk overlooking differences when we move towards the transversal. Yet, the risks are worth taking. Canada is itself an experiment in a larger project across time and space. We have a federal government that binds us together beyond our provincial life. We have a railroad that our forbearers labored to create so as to connect us all together. We have a national psyche that is as large as this land that stretches form sea to sea to sea. We have a national history, varied and mixed, full of achievements and failings, but which is truly ours. Within the province of Quebec, where the movement for separation still lingers, there resides among many a general appreciation for the Canadian project. Given all this, I think that we can articulate a general notion of a Canadian spirituality and promote it as a national educational project. Bringing the contemplative-in-action method to bear upon our national soul can help to achieve this goal.

The reservations to incorporating spiritual education within our schools can also be rooted in the resistance to religion in the secular state. In particular there can be resistance to having spirituality included with our public education system fearing that this would simply be acquiescing to the religious realm. However, one of the myths about Canadian education is that secular education is the great leveler and that all religious traditions can healthily exist within the secular pluralist state if they accept the silencing of their voices within the public domain and remain peripheral to the centering motif of democratic capitalism. Moving towards intentionally incorporating the spiritual dimension within Canadian schools need not necessarily mean the admission of or dismissal of a theistic or religious meaning system. Nor should it be seen as necessarily undermining the collective project of educating the Canadian citizen of today and the future. It might simply lead to greater truth telling and cooperation between the two streams of educational thought presently flowing through Canada.

There can also be resistance to spiritual education within faith-based schools. Such resistance can be based in a mistrust of spirituality, particularly mystical and political spirituality, which is often unjustly perceived as highly subjective and potentially divisive. Mysticism can frequently challenge the objectives and dogmatic confines of religion. Methods for teaching spirituality in faith-based schools are often only tolerated and rarely fully endorsed by authority figures who are often mandated to hold doctrinal lines to ensure the identity of the particular schools. Still, the mystical traditions found within all world religions are wells of spiritual wisdom, which, if tapped into, would benefit the religious education being offered today.

Including spirituality within Canadian education would provide a way to prepare the young to embrace their citizenship within Canada not only as an opportunity but also as a responsibility to the collective. It would be about opening the minds and hearts of the young to the possibility of a soulful life within Canada, to the possibility of a civic engagement that requires the integration of the national and the personal consciousness, and to the possibility of belonging to a community of communities. Such a project would move the educational agenda to a level beyond simple knowledge acquisition and skill development as preparation for gainful employment and consumerism. It would bring education to a different place, a soulful place, where one might better recognize the many rivers that run through and across Canada. It would be to educate for the many streams of life that flow across our land and for an appreciation that, while these rivers continue to flow unceasingly, the sea is never full.

Opting to include civic spirituality within Canadian education as a middle path between religious and secular systems will meet with some resistance, particularly by those who dismiss spirituality as a subject matter in itself. Beyond the disagreements concerning theistic and non-theistic spiritualities lays a lack of agreement concerning the spiritual capacity of the human person. Simply put, is there spiritual knowledge born from a spiritual way of knowing? Let us turn our attention to these questions for they are relevant to our entire proposal to include civic spirituality within our Canadian education systems.

NOTES

1. John Ralston Saul, "Peace, Fairness and Good Government" Part II in *A Fair Country: Telling Truths About Canada* (Toronto: Viking Canada, 2008), pp. 111–169.
2. Ibid., pp. 244–250.
3. Ibid., pp. 3–107.
4. Peter C. Emberley and Waller R. Newell, *Bankrupt Education: The Decline of Liberal Education in Canada* (Toronto: University of Toronto Press, 1994), p. 137.
5. Ibid., pp. 156–158.
6. Mark G. McGowan, *The Enduring Gift: Catholic Education in the Province of Ontario* (Toronto: Ontario Catholic Schools Trustee's Association, 2001), p. 1.
7. Ibid., pp. 2–3.
8. Jane Jacobs, *Dark Age Ahead* (Toronto: Vintage Canada, 2005).
9. Charles Taylor, *A Secular Age* (Cambridge, MA: The Belknap Press of Harvard University Press, 2007).
10. For an insightful analysis of the connection between meaning and spirituality, see Viktor E. Frankl's *Man's Search for Ultimate Meaning* (Cambridge, MA: Perseus Publishing, 2000).
11. Neil Postman, *The End of Education: Redefining The Value of School* (New York: Vintage Books, 1996).
12. Lois Sweet, *God in the Classroom* (Toronto: McClelland & Stewart, 1997), p. 222.
13. Paul Ricoeur, *Lectures on Ideology and Utopia* (New York: Columbia University Press, 1986), pp. 230–235. Ricoeur argues that religion, while susceptible to ideological moments, does provide critique of the prevailing social ideologies, particularly of the market and technology.
14. Sweet, *God in the Classroom*, pp. 240–245.
15. For examples of current research in the area of spirituality and education see: *The Heart of Learning: Spirituality in Education*, ed. Steven Glazer (New York, NY: Tracher/Putnam, 1999) and *Holistic Learning and Spirituality in Education: Breaking New Ground*, ed. John P. Miller (Albany, NY: SUNY Press, 2005).
16. See: John P. Miller, *The Holistic Teacher* (Toronto: OISE Press, 1993); *The Contemplative Practitioner: Meditation in Education and the Professions* (Toronto: OISE Press, 1994); *Education and the Soul: Toward a Spiritual Curriculum* (Albany, NY: SUNY Press, 2000); *Educating for Wisdom and Compassion: Creating Conditions for Timeless Learning* (Thousand Oaks, California: Corwin Press, 2006).
17. *Developing the Inner Life and Changing the World: The Spiritual Care and Guidance and Community Involvement Service*, Gouvernement du Québec: Ministère

de l'Education, du Loisir et du Sport, 2006. http://www.mels.gouv.qc.ca/DGFJ/csc/asec/pdf/26–0001–A.pdf

18. Clive Beck, "Religious and Spiritual Education" in *Better Schools: A Values Perspective* (New York, NY: The Falmer Press, 1990), pp. 157–174.

19. The retrieval of the traditional concept of the soul seems to resonate with our culture. Indeed, Thomas Moore's *Care of the Soul: A Guide for Cultivating Depth and Sacredness in Everyday Life* (New York, NY: Harper Collins, 1992) was not only a best-seller but also opened up new areas for public discourse about issues of the soul and spirituality in our time.

Chapter Two

Foundations of Spiritual Knowing

Then one day I was walking along Tinker Creek thinking of nothing at all and I saw the tree with the lights in it. I saw the backyard cedar where the mourning doves roost charged and transfigured, each cell buzzing with flame. I stood on the grass with the lights in it, grass that was wholly fire, utterly focused and utterly dreamed. It was less like seeing than like being for the first time seen, knocked breathless by a powerful glance. The flood of fire abated, but I'm still spending the power. ... I have since only very rarely seen the tree with the lights in it. The vision comes and goes, mostly goes, but I live for it...[1]

The first time I traveled into the heart of the Canadian landscape was in 1978. I had a summer job working on an exploratory drilling crew looking for uranium seventy miles into the bush from Uranium City, Saskatchewan. The journey in itself was an awakening. I took a train from Ottawa to Winnipeg, which almost took two days. Then I took a train from Winnipeg to Le Pas, Manitoba where I spent a few days with friends. I remember that train ride north of Winnipeg because as we crossed the eastern edge of the Canadian prairies the early May sun held its position in the sky well past 10:00 p.m. The wondrous landscape rolled by my window and I could only marvel at the beauty. From Le Pas, I traveled by car to Flin Flon where I stayed for a few days, checked in with the drilling company and waited for our departure into the bush.

A few days later, I joined a small crew and we drove by truck from Flin Flon to L'Orange, Saskatchewan. The dirt road, covered with mud from a recent downpour, was riddled with potholes, making the journey there a raucous one. From L'Orange, we boarded a Cessna and flew to Uranium City. The flight over the northern part of Saskatchewan was wonderful. In contrast to the flat, open prairies that I had seen as I traveled north of Winnipeg, the landscape was full of hundreds of small lakes and rivers and the land was covered with short coniferous trees giving the landscape a dark green hue. This was quite a surprise to me, for I had not expected such vast territory to have so much fresh water or to be so beautiful. From Uranium City, I was flown into the bush by helicopter and deposited, with gear and supplies, on a ridge that would be the location of our drilling camp for the summer.

The work was long, hard and dangerous. The most memorable moments came to me during the night shift. I reveled in the opportunities that came to climb the 25–foot mast above the drilling deck where I would have to stand while we changed the drilling rods that we sent into the rock below as we drilled for uranium. At our northern position during the summer nights the sun never fully receded, but always left a bit of a halo in the distance. I loved to look out at the horizon and watch the haloed sun silhouette the jack pines, but I particularly loved those nights when the Northern Lights would dance, in all their cascading beauty, across the edge of sight and darkness. Alone at the top of the mast, watching those lights turn and twist the dark sky into a deep and rich beauty, while below me lay the harsh and rugged terrain of the muskeg, I felt a deep sense of awe and wonder at the pristine beauty of nature. The beauty of the land, the different textures of the day and night skies, and the smell and feel of the earth gradually, after numerous trips up the mast, left me with a deep sense of peace and communion. At that point in my life I had spent four years at university studying the humanities, had a head full of ideas and thought of myself as somewhat learned. There, however, while standing at the top of the mast and hanging in the dark sky I slowly began to listen to my own heart, to observe the movement of the dim light across the horizon, and to sense the wind as it passed over the muskeg. Ever so slowly, a sense of respect and humility filled me and I felt a softening of my heart. Slowly, I remembered another way of knowing, one that I had first experienced as a child while walking in the fields of France. That way of knowing is a way that is deeply connected to nature and is a way of knowing that arises from the body when all the senses are open and engaged. My time in northern Saskatchewan, when I was awakened by nature to the reality of a different kind of knowledge, one not taught in school and university, has stayed with me over the years, providing ballast as I've journeyed through life. Those weeks in the heart of Canada's wilderness were pure gift and provided me with an insight into the necessity of paying attention to all ways of seeking and learning, especially the ways of spiritual knowing.

Experiences such as these have led me to the conviction that spiritual education can be a middle path between secular and faith-based streams of education in Canada. This belief is rooted in experiences of spiritual knowing and experiences of what I would identify as the Canadian soul. It is also rooted in my experience as an educator and a chaplain who follows the contemplative-in-action method for spirituality, a method found in both world religions and philosophy, which forms an appropriate pedagogical tool for Canadian spiritual education. Before exploring the content and method of spiritual education in Canada, we need to attend to a more fundamental question, which will be of particular concern for educators. That is, is there such a thing as a spiritual way of knowing that yields spiritual knowledge or insights? This question is fundamental to following a middle way through the often-fractious debate between secular and faith-based philosophies of education. I shall argue that there is indeed a spiritual way of knowing other than the present paradigm that dominates Canadian education today. This way is deeper, more intuitive, affective, and comprehensive in scope. It is a way rooted in experience, both personal and collective. It is the way of wisdom, of love, and of the soul.

More and more Western educational theorists and practitioners, both secular and religious,[2] are acknowledging the necessary task of educating for a spiritual life. Indeed, among secular philosophers of education there is a growing awareness that the intentional exclusion of religion and spirituality within public education has contributed to the impoverishment of the enterprise of learning. Clive Beck and John P. Miller from the University of Toronto and Michael Volkey from the University of British Columbia, as well as Nel Noddings and Parker Palmer[3] from the United States, are educational theorists who advocate for a recovery of spirituality within public education today. The call for such a recovery lies in the recognition that any education that claims to pursue excellence but ignores the spiritual dimension of life is an education that is incomplete because spirituality, understood in its primal sense as the search for meaning, is a constitutive part of what it means to be human and hence requires inclusion in our educational practice.

In addition to this growing recognition amongst secular education theorists, there is also a growing awareness among philosophers of religious education that there is a need to foster spirituality as well as education in a religious worldview.[4] Indeed, there is slowly emerging amongst religious educators a recognition of the changing role of traditional religions within Canada's growing secular and pluralist culture, and that they need to respond appropriately to this change. Part of their response is to tap into the spiritual paths found within religion and to expose students to these insights to complement religious teachings, practices, and morals.

There appears, then, to be a converging awareness between both secular and religious educators that Canadian education today requires the inclusion of spirituality, one that responds to the needs of individuals and communities at large. My own experience has been that these points of convergence between religious and secular approaches are often visible through their mutual actions for justice, peace, and ecological sustainability. That is, when students and teachers join together in common humanitarian or ecological actions we often recognize a spark of deep concern for life that has led us to work together for the betterment of our world. This deep concern arises from the realm of the soul. Religious and secular educators and students may have different motives for their common action, but such common actions serve to verify the authenticity of these differing spiritual motivations.

While secular and religious educators agree that an education for spirituality is an imperative for our times,[5] most would also agree that seeking to educate for spirituality within Canada's educational systems is very difficult. This difficulty is due not only to the lack of a shared approach to spiritual education, part of which I am trying to address in these reflections. It is also due to the lack of shared language and symbols regarding spirituality in a secular and pluralistic age. We need language and symbols to amplify, communicate, and teach this spirituality for without language and symbols, the experiences and spiritual insights are lost. More importantly, though, is the fact that Canadian schools, as in other Western nations, promote knowledge as a way to gain control of the world rather than knowledge as a way to live in harmony with the world. This is particularly problematic since harmony and communion are central ingredients of a spiritual life. The truth is that Canadian education practice today is deeply rooted in our Western post-Enlightenment fascination with intellectual knowledge and coupled with a championing of scientific and technological ways of learning. This approach to education is a reflection of our secular cultural fixation with science and technology as well as the pursuit of wealth and power. A spiritual education that promotes living in harmony with and in service to the world is rooted in an alternative, yet complementary, way of knowing. It is an approach to knowing that is often marginalized and muted within Canadian education. Should we be able to explore the gifts and limits of each way of knowing and embrace a more cooperative association of both ways, we can hope that our education will be comprehensive and hence more responsive to the needs of our time.

THE WAY OF KNOWING AS CONTROL

I am reminded here of an incident that happened during my teaching training which has stayed with me over the years, mostly because it points to the difference between these two ways of knowing. I was sitting in a large lecture hall and the professor at the front of the hundreds of student teachers made the following comment to support his advocacy of the need to be clear and rigorous in our evaluation of learning. We needed to use a taxonomy of clear and objective learning skills, content, and goals. He said, "Well, we can't just all sit around quietly, hold hands, and intuit!" At this point, the entire hall burst out into nervous laughter. As one who appreciates the importance of quiet and relationships as mediums for learning and who respects the intuitive function, I remember saying to myself, "Well, why not?" The reason, as I quickly came to see during my initial years in teaching, was that we as professionals have been unable to come up with acceptable methods for evaluating other ways of knowing, ways that include intuition, creativity, character, values, and the emotions. There have been some attempts to establish a taxonomy of affective learning and values within education. In recent years, some provinces, such as Ontario, Quebec, and Alberta, have devoted attention to character development and civic virtues in the primary and intermediate levels of schooling. Such attempts have met resistance within the mainstream of educational practice. One of the reasons for this resistance is that these ways of knowing, while real, are often intangible, highly subjective, and very fluid. They resist the hard exactitude and concreteness required for objective verification, judgment and categorization, which are the strengths of the scientific method. It is difficult to complete a written test that can then be scored by some school or ministerial scrutinizer. In a culture like ours that prizes objective and practical knowledge, it is no wonder that a movement in these areas has been difficult to sustain.

Canadian education, like in most Western countries, is overwhelmingly influenced by our modern, post-Enlightenment project of disconnected rationalism, which champions the supremacy of reason and the autonomy of the individual in the pursuit and creation of knowledge. Thus, the knowledge that is considered valuable is knowledge that is reasonable and practical. The educated person is the autonomous individual who successfully accumulates reams and reams of rational knowledge that can be applied in pragmatic ways. This ability to accumulate leads to an approach to education in which we reward those with intellectual and pragmatic knowledge as more intelligent than poetic, intuitive and spiritual knowledge. This approach is a far cry from the Greek approach to education as the turning of the soul away from darkness of ignorance into the light of self-knowledge, as the basis for living the good life and serving others in society.

In our mainstream educational philosophy, thinking takes precedence over all other ways of knowing (sensory, experiential, affective, intuitive, relational, communal, and participatory). In this context, cognitive knowledge is what separates one from the *other* (whether the *other* is a person, nature or a subject matter), gives one power and control over one's world. Moreover, under this championing of intellectual knowledge the priority is given to the individual as a knower rather than what is known in community.[6] The goal here is individual power, giving rise to the oft-heard creed: knowledge is power.

This education of vaulted rationalism gives rise to an understanding of a student as one who is an autonomous individual capable of thinking, primarily alone, with the view of mastering content by developing critical thinking skills. Hence, students learn content that can be memorized, categorized, applied, and tested by the teacher. We have witnessed a deepening of this approach to learning in recent years as ministries of education across Canada have stridently promoted centralized curriculum, standardized testing, and ranking of school performance. This move has been in response to concerns regarding Canadian competitiveness in the global economy. When the last wave of advocacy for learning by objectives and standardized testing swept through the Western world during the Eighties and Nineties, Canadian decision makers were moved to ensure Canada's reputation in education and adopted policy changes that fixated educational practice on objective benchmarks. Mathematics, science, English, and computer studies ascended higher in priority than ever before. Such directives served intellectual, scientific and technological education but mostly sidelined other ways of knowing within Canadian education. It needs to be noted here that the main motive for this strident adoption of standardized testing and learning by objectives was the perception that Canada was lagging behind other countries in terms of our education and that this lag was negatively impacting upon our global competitiveness and our standard of living. While economic concerns certainly need to be part of the goals of education, any education system that allows itself to be driven by a purely economic vision of the human person is a system that forfeits its core mission which is to turn the soul of the student to the life of the world, a life which is much more than simply the economy. This move to align the goals and strategies of education with a limited vision of the human person as essentially an economic animal has contributed to the drift away from the heart of teaching, which is to turn the soul to the world.

Regrettably the philosophy of education that has overtaken our Canadian education systems is rooted in an economic view of personhood coupled with the Enlightenment championing of the intellect. We should note that, as discussed earlier, it was not the intended purpose of education when Canada was created. Back then, a more organic and communal approach to education was advocated, one that saw the goal of the educated citizen to include a duty and obligation to care for oneself but also for others in the commonweal. It is perhaps difficult to pinpoint when and why the shift in purpose took place. Was it during the post-World War II boom? Was it due to the influence of American economic policies upon Canada? Was it due to the shrinking of borders during globalization? Regardless of the cause and time, it is clear that the notion of education as organically connected to the common good has been eclipsed by an Enlightenment approach to education that values individualism and autonomy more than community and interdependence and an economic goal that highlights wealth, consumption, and social status more than service and the common good.

In our current approach to education, any attention to relational knowing is primarily between the student and the teacher. The understanding that a student learns through a community of persons gets short shrift within the knowledge-as-power approach to learning. The view of knowledge as power is reinforced by the exercise of power in which the teacher, through the use of judgment, distributes power to students via the allocation of marks. Reducing the goal of learning to levels of achievement, with corresponding marks, ultimately results in the commoditization of learning wherein knowledge is studied, appropriated, and expressed all within a hierarchy of value that can be exchanged for privilege and power. Knowledge is pursued then for its instrumental value rather than its intrinsic value. This approach is followed from primary to post-secondary education resulting in a citizenry equipped with the expectation that knowledge is for power and economic gain. Obviously, such a way of educating provides a poor foundation for spiritual education, which focuses on other values such as relatedness, community, wisdom, service and love.

A critical distinction between rational and spiritual ways of knowing lies in differing motivations for pursuing knowledge. Within the modern Enlightenment view of education, knowledge is possessed mostly for its instrumental value. Thus, the questions become: "What is this knowledge good for?"' and "How does this knowledge work in the real world?" Instrumental learning frequently results in the often-heard question in the classroom: "Will it be on the exam?" What teacher, who is in love with his or her subject matter, does not die a little each time they hear this question, a question which undermines the intrinsic value they find in the subject? In our current approach we rarely seek knowledge for its intrinsic value. As the eminent Canadian philosopher Charles Taylor argues, it is instrumental reason wherein "maximum efficiency, the best cost-output ratio, is its measure of success"[7] that is lauded today. Pragmatism and utility give knowledge its value within contemporary education, especially when applied to scientific and technological knowledge.

To say that the post-Enlightenment championing of rational and scientific knowledge drives our current approach to education is not to say that this approach permits no room for other ways of learning and knowing. There is indeed an appreciation for the role of imagination and creativity in education,[8] particularly within the arts and humanities, and an appreciation for the role of experience within some disciplines. There are many ways in which the relational and communal dimensions of personhood are nurtured and re-inforced within the rhythm of the life cycle of schooling. In reality, however, these approaches are often merely tolerated to the extent that they reinforce the acquisition of knowledge as power. They are more likely marginalized from our main focus of acquiring instrumental knowledge. We witness this tolerance and marginalization for these alternative ways of knowing when we see art, music, and drama, not to mention the traditional humanity subjects of history and social studies, constantly fighting for inclusion in the curriculum, in programs, and in budgets. At best, the collective value of these approaches lies in their usefulness in supporting the hegemony of instrumental rational-ism and scientific technology. Teachers, particularly at the secondary level, who teach non-compulsory, elective subjects often face greater discipline challenges in the classroom because students are often not motivated, or con-trolled, by the requirement to gain a certain mark in order to pass and gradu-ate. The objective and instrumentalist approach of the power pedagogy tends to stifle the inner motivation to learn contributing to a lack of self-mastery and personal confidence, which often translates into disengagement from the community of the classroom. The instrumental approach to education has definite repercussions in the classroom.

Our cultural bias in favor of science, rationalism and instrumental reason is simply part of our Western fascination with knowledge as power. What it does is eclipse the concerns of spirituality within Canadian education and undermine any attempts to facilitate a nationally responsive approach to spiritual life. This bias should not surprise us because spirituality is focused much more on the intrinsic value of knowledge rather than its instrumen-tal value. Thus, in the spiritual way of knowing, the concern is with what knowledge can teach me, not with what I can do or how much power I will gain by acquiring the knowledge. The motivation for seeking spiritual knowledge is with how such knowledge will help to shape the identity and person of the learner rather than how the learner will use that knowledge to shape the world. Spiritual education is about the formation of the student as a whole person. These are two very different motivations. One way sees knowledge in itself as valuable in that, once appropriated, it helps to en-lighten me and assist me in living in and caring for the world. In this view, I learn so as to be able to live and to serve others and the world. In this sense, knowledge uses me as I journey through life. The other way, the way of the pure intellect, sees knowledge as important for personal power so that I can control my presence in the world and hence control the world itself. Here, I use my knowledge to make my way in the world. The ego, rather than the heart, is fed via the way of knowledge as power while the soul is fed via the spiritual way of knowing. Quite obviously the best approach to education would be one in which the ego and the heart, the intellect and the soul are all nurtured together.

There are many examples of how knowledge as power is operative throughout our Canadian education systems. Not only do we see it in our recent move towards benchmarks and standardized testing, we also see it in how we construct our schools, manage our education systems, and chart our paths of learning. Indeed, as Donald Oliver and Kathleen Gershman have argued, the root metaphor of the machine,[9] which drives our Western culture, also drives our schools. This machine metaphor is manifest in structuring our curriculum around specialization and fragmentation. The division of knowledge into subject disciplines is as old as the first philosophers. In our time, the specialization of knowledge within various subjects has led to a situation where teachers and learners learn more and more about one specific field but little about how different subject fields relate. Our ever-increasing focus on specialization has led to a growing fragmenting of the curriculum and of teaching faculties. We see this fragmentation more clearly in secondary and post-secondary faculties where teachers and professors are hired precisely because they possess specialized qualifications. This approach is not automatically wrong, but it is definitely shortsighted when viewed from a spiritual point of view. From a spiritual frame, where the focus is on commonalities and unifying knowledge and action, specialization with fragmentation is counter-productive.

For Oliver, the consequence of technical knowing is a fragmented view of reality and a fragmentation of the educational project itself.[10] Building upon an ever-increasing dissection of knowledge, learning becomes an experience of increasing fragmentation with little capacity for synthesis and connection. We continue to create and manage our education systems based on the modern orientation towards fragmenting and with an unconscious allegiance to the machine metaphor driving our educational decisions. Witness the burgeoning of academic disciplines, departments, and the championing of specialization within modern education. Witness the growth of huge urban high schools and overcrowded colleges and universities. Moreover, look at the emphasis upon education as preparation for work that has taken over the educational policies of many North American jurisdictions. Creating workers for the multifaceted global economy has become the rationale for schools, colleges, and universities today. As Jane Jacobs has argued in her book *Dark Age Ahead*, much of education today has become merely the pursuit of credentials so as to ensure one's marketability in an every changing economy.[11] Indeed, fragmentation, specialization, and credentialism are common features of education today.

The contemporary push towards fragmentation merely reflects the lack of any common ground as a result of a deconstructive postmodern distrust of

universal narratives or appeals to unity. Indeed, some have argued that attempts to universalize are simply thinly veiled attempts to dominate others.[12]
While there is merit to this critique, especially as a corrective to totalitarian
systems of thought, the result of breaking free from a common ground has
been increased difference, incommensurability, and fragmentation, as well as
a dismissal of the capacity to effectively engage the concerns which effect
Canadians as a whole. The consequence of the fragmentation that marks today's Canadian society and education is the dissipation of creative energy and
a diminishment of Canadian identity. When difference and specialization are
relentlessly pursued under the metaphor of a machine and without any centering common ground, the result is a deterioration of relatedness, meaning, and
community, which impacts negatively on the life of Canadians. As a result,
the energy that results from the discovery of knowledge tends to dissipate and
become lost because it cannot be shared with others or focused towards the
common good. What results from increasing specialization without a common ground is analogous to orbital decay whereby an object in orbit, because
its connection to the center is disturbed, begins to move out of the tension
between centrifugal and centripetal forces that have been keeping it in orbit.
Eventually, the object either falls to earth or flies off into deep space.

    This may all sound very theoretical to the front-line teacher. However,
think of the effects of such a learning environment upon the student. While
there are many students who come to us who are eager, confident, and tal-
ented, there are just as many who arrive who are discouraged and wounded.
Is it no wonder then that the wounded and struggling students have to work
so hard to succeed in school? They are already broken and traveling with
a deficit. Then they come into our schools that operate like factories with
fractured components and little cohesion. Such a learning environment does
little to support the limited or wounded learner. Moments that highlight the
communal and the relational provide meaning and support for students.

    Indeed, think of how important are community events in the life a school.
The break from the routine, the showcasing of talent, the working together
to support a common event or goal, all aid in breaking down the fragmenting
forces within schooling today. These events point to the need for communal
identity and purpose; to the need for a shared focus or a common ground that
connects students and teachers within a school culture. Spirit days are practical exercises in attending to the communal and spiritual dimensions within
education. My own observation is that it is a wise principal who knows how
to pace the inclusion of such events in the school year so as to maintain the
rhythm between focused concentration required for learning and creative fun
required for growing and living in community.

Modern education, so widely influenced by the Enlightenment project of disconnected rationalism and the machine metaphor, serves Canadian culture at large with its focus on power, wealth accumulation, and status. It is clear to many though that we have reached the limits of this modern approach to education. Indeed, reducing education to the appropriation of instrumental and pragmatic knowledge, while uncritically accepting the machine metaphor for life and social construction, does not necessarily provide us with citizens equipped with the consciousness needed to rise to the challenges of our time. The emerging recognition of our need to pay attention to spirituality within education is one example of our current quest for meaning, relationship, wisdom, and community. Essentially, the recognition of the need for spirituality in education is a manifestation of our need and desire to move beyond the limits of modern educational philosophy with its limited focus on knowledge as power.

Ultimately, the knowledge-as-power approach to education results in a depleted sense of meaning and a diminished spiritual life. It feeds on the illusion that we are in control of the world, directing its affairs and unaccountable, except to our vaulted intellect. This way drives our education system and creates generations of citizens who are exposed to only one way of knowledge. Intellectual knowledge divorced from intuition, imagination, feeling, aesthetics, values, and relationships is incomplete knowledge. Such an approach leads people to know only partially, not wholly. It is as if people were asked to breathe with one lung when they were created with two. This partial or incomplete knowledge is the result of not including the other dimension of knowledge, the way of spiritual knowing.

SPIRITUALITY AS A WAY OF KNOWING

If we are to know fully what it means to be human and if education has a role in the formation of citizens capable of fully engaging the challenges and opportunities of our time, it is then imperative that we pursue a holistic and comprehensive approach to learning. To do so, we need to go beyond the limits of the rational knowledge pursued within a power paradigm to include the spiritual knowledge paradigm that places knowledge at the service of the soul. We need to reclaim our spiritual, soulful way of knowing, a way of knowing closely aligned with the heart. This pursuit is a way of knowing deeply rooted in our fundamental nature as creatures living and breathing on this beautiful and fragile planet. It is a way in which we remain open to the mysterious *more* that permeates existence.

From our experience of living with, in, and through the created world, which forms the conditions for our thriving, we know that there is a creative and dynamic energy that flows through the world and through all creatures of the world. Plato called this energy the *anima mundi* or the soul of the world.[13] This *anima mundi* unites what is separate[14] and forms the conditions for the many diverse expressions of life in our world. The human person, when walking in natural surroundings, knows experientially, through sensory awareness that they coexist with this *anima mundi* or soul of the world. They feel intimately connected to nature and come to know that their wellbeing is directly connected to the soul of the world. It is often accompanied by feelings of awe, wonder, and gratitude. Some philosophers have called this deep, intimate, connected way of knowing "co-natural knowing."[15]

Co-natural knowledge is knowledge acquired when a person has an experience of being *at-one-with* reality. It includes an experiential and intuitive awareness of inner and outer worlds as connected, and of the absence of any dualistic separation between objective and subjective states of awareness. We see this co-natural or spiritual knowledge in its primal form in the life of an infant. Most infants experience little or no separation between their ego and the external reality of the world. The inner world and the outer world are not differentiated but rather experienced as one. Most infants are peaceful, harmonious, and full of awe when their needs are being met in the real world through the actions of adults or other caregivers. Such knowledge, which is a knowledge of being loved and valued, is essential to life, for without it we die, sometimes physically, sometimes emotionally. When there is a communion of needs and desires between an infant and the world a feeling of harmony and peace results. When children do not experience the *others* of the world as responsive to their needs they cry out for attention. This way of co-natural knowing is essential to the life of personhood, for as Erikson has pointed out, a person who is not loved at the beginning of their life struggles to trust the innate goodness of life as they grow. Indeed, the infant who has experienced peace and harmony develops the capacity for wonder and awe as they grow. While this consciousness is primarily a needs-based consciousness, one that falls away as we grow in ego consciousness and awareness of the needs of others, it nonetheless points to a fundamental way of knowing encoded within human consciousness. Such a way of knowing, of being at one with reality is a spiritual way of knowing.

This spiritual way of knowing is often awakened throughout our life when we are in love. Indeed, lovers may be able to explain conceptually their reasons for being in love, but the knowledge of love is an experiential one shared through body, emotions, imagination, and intuition. We find this way of knowing as well in those relationships we have with kindred spirits or soul friends, those who support us and love us, often in non-romantic ways. The co-natural way of knowing, which is essentially about communion and harmony, is a spiritual way of knowing. Through this way of knowing a person learns to attend to one's self, others and the soul of the world together. Spiritual knowing in this sense involves being at one with the soul of the world and experiencing one's wellbeing and one's life as connected to the world's soul.

The fruits of spiritual knowing are peace, harmony, awe, and wonderment, which often arise from a sense of the presence of *more* beyond our scientific, philosophical, religious and sensory views of the world. For a Canadian voice of this natural and innate spiritual knowing, we need simply turn to Sharon Butala. Butala, in her autobiographical work *The Perfection of the Morning*, reflects deeply on her years of living on the Saskatchewan prairies and describes her numinous experiences of communion with the land, the animals, and the grasses of the prairies. She laments the fact that such experiences, which are so often overlooked in the scientific worldview and usually delegated to the voices of poets and artists, risk being forgotten because we do not have the language to communicate them.

> I think we have so allowed the scientific approach to the world to take over our perceptions that we are afraid to mention such experiences for fear of being laughed at or vilified. When we do, we find ourselves stammering, struggling for words, never being able to convey in language to our own satisfaction exactly what it felt like or looked like or what sensations it evoked in us. We struggle against skepticism, our own as much as anyone else's, and in time we lapse into silence about them and a whole, valuable dimension of human experience remains unsung and unvalidated.[16]

For Butala, the experience of being in nature lends itself to mystical knowing, a way of knowing in which we are at one with nature, and from which we feel a sense of belonging to a world that "is more wonderful than any of us have dared to guess, as all great poets have been telling us since the invention of poetry."[17] Such knowledge can, as Annie Dillard claims, provide us with a vision from which to live. Co-natural, or spiritual knowledge often results in an amplification of the awareness of the "benignity at the heart of the universe, the sense of meaning, the ultimate graciousness of life."[18] It is essentially a mystical way of knowing. Such knowing leads to wonder, gratitude, playfulness, creativity, and a sense of being at home in the universe. It adds to a sense of meaning, an appreciation of community, an ascent to mystery, and an ability to embrace paradox in life. These are all worthy capacities to be encouraged in any program in spiritual education.

If we are initiated into this way of attending to and living from the world soul that is present in all creation, we are then able to tap into a deep experiential well that yields harmony, meaning, love, awe, connection, mystery, and energy. Spiritual learning requires that we pursue a holistic approach to life, one where we deliberately attend to the soul present in the created world. What this attention requires is that we understand spirituality as being grounded upon, and oriented towards, what psychologists and philosophers call a soulful life. Attending to the soul, present in both the world and the person, and mediated through culture and institutions, is foundational to spiritual knowing and is a cornerstone to spiritual education. If we are to educate for a healthy spirituality we must begin with trying to amplify an appreciation of our original being at one with the created world and the cosmos.

In this spiritual, co-natural way of knowing one seeks the "hidden centrum"[19] that grounds the universe. This seeking is an action of the person who wants to grow in the awareness of the underlying unity that permeates all of creation. Seeking spiritual knowledge does not withdraw one from the world into introspection.[20] Rather, such spirituality requires an outward, active focus in which one seeks to behold the hidden ground or soul present in the world and to allow one to live and act in accordance with this soul. Such a way of knowing does not discount the reality of diversity and difference that characterizes our postmodern world. On the contrary, spiritual knowing recognizes that such diversity is a natural consequence of the creative energy that is found in the unity of the universe itself. What a spiritual person seeks to maintain is an awareness of the fundamental unity of life in the midst of diversity and differences. Such awareness buffers the forces that often propel us towards endless fragmentation, disconnection, and alienation.

A spiritual person who seeks the soul in life tries to avoid excessive abstraction. The famous Trappist monk Thomas Merton recognized the tendency of much of our intellectual tradition to reside in excessive abstractions as an essential problematic for our times.[21] Spiritual knowing does not look kindly on dislocated abstractions or the pursuit of intellectual knowledge divorced from real life. Indeed, Clive Beck has argued that we must attend to everyday life and include the active areas of life within spirituality for it to be healthy.[22] Essentially, students of the spiritual life neither seek to acquire knowledge for the sake of power nor to avoid real life through abstractions, but rather to be engaged in the world and allow oneself to be used by the knowledge they have learned so as to co-create with the soul of the world. Spiritual education, then, requires that we move beyond concerns of power, status, and wealth, which are often the primary concerns of our prevailing approach to education, towards the promotion of knowledge so as to grow in service to others and the world.

An eminent American teacher, writer, and public intellectual in the area of spirituality, Parker Palmer, has advocated that spirituality must include the active life of social action. He argues that the tendency within Western spirituality to fall back upon a monastic practice of interiority, silence, solitude, and balance is at odds with our modern world that values extroversion, achievement, changing structures, and striving to improve the world through transformative action. While aware that many social activists do not live with interior freedom, Palmer still values the place of the active life as a necessary expression of one's spiritual energy.[23] Others have argued that education for spirituality today must include both the inner life of the individual and the active life to work for social change.[24] Bringing the social and political into our personal spiritual horizon of meaning is the primary need of our day. Indeed, the social and political framework of our life together as Canadians needs to be included as a core ingredient in our Canadian civic spirituality.

In order to meet this need, Robert McAfee Brown has argued that we need to move beyond the "great fallacy of dualism"[25] wherein we separate the active and contemplative dimensions of life. We need to move beyond the concerns of good and bad, male and female, secular and religious, oppressor and victim, to a new way of living, one that focuses on our common areas of concern: justice, peace, environmental sustainability, inclusivity, and cooperation. Such a move does not necessarily discount the concerns of differences but rather situates differences under a larger ethic, the pursuit of the common good through which we all live and thrive. A healthy and holistic Canadian spirituality would require that we engage in shared actions that help to repair and transform the world, eradicate the conflicts and injustices that exist, and build inclusive and cooperative communities.

Education for spirituality, then, must include skills to increase our attentiveness to the fullness of reality as well as the skills needed to help us serve as cooperators with the world soul for the transformation and healing of the world. It must include developing the skills and talents that contribute to our own personal good and to the national soul found with others. Ultimately, spirituality must also include the active, communal and political dimensions of life as well as the personal, reflective and interior dimensions if it is to be credible. Essentially, in order to educate for a responsible civic spirituality today, Canadian educators need to align the development of personal interiority along with actions that promote the social and environmental good. Educating students in this manner will assist them in becoming full citizens, capable of intelligently and respectfully living in harmony with the soul of the world.

CONNECTING THE TWO WAYS OF KNOWING

The way of intellectual knowing and the way of spiritual knowing are not at odds. Quite the contrary, they are best learned together, for they are mutually beneficial. Just as two lungs provide for better breathing than one does, engaging in both ways of knowing provides for our best learning. In truth, difficulties arise when we pursue one way at the expense of the other, or when one way is valued more than the other.

If we are honest with ourselves, we will recognize that the pursuit of intellectual knowledge for the purposes of acquiring power is the driving force in our education system today. This recognition should not surprise us, for it reflects the values of our Canadian culture today with its focus on wealth, independence, and prestige. These values mirror those of our neighbours to the south who hold as central to their national narrative the freedom of the autonomous individual. Canadians need to recall that our nation was formed along a more communal and organic vision of society, one that has been eroded over the years due to outside forces. The gradual erosion of our communal understanding of personhood has contributed to the loss of our national soul. We are at a point in our history where the paradigm of knowledge for the sake of power can no longer serve us. Indeed, we need to reclaim the importance of a spiritual, soulful, communal way of knowing. What is required now is a rediscovery of the spiritual way of knowing, a humbling of the intellectual way of knowing as power, and a return to a balance between these two ways. Only with a recovery of a more holistic approach to learning can we hope to learn the ways and means to handle the immense challenges that face us as a nation.

How are we to achieve this balanced and more holistic way? Let me lay out three considerations. First, we need to recognize the harm done by exclusively pursuing the knowledge-as-power paradigm in education. Once we begin to humbly recognize this potential for harm, we can then consciously make decisions to move away from the sole pursuit of this way of educating. This change will also require a period of unlearning, which will not necessarily be easy or painless. In the spiritual life, one often has to unlearn what one has learned in order to be transformed. This unlearning, this purging of prior knowledge, can be painful, and is one of the reasons why a truly authentic spirituality is so often resisted. The spiritual path is not always pain free. The purging of the lauded role of the intellect in learning can lead to humility, which is an important attitude to nourish in life. Purging and unlearning what we held to be so important does not necessarily discount the significance of that knowledge. We are the grateful inheritors of a vast store of knowledge and we stand on the shoulders of those who have gone before us. A recognition of the social cost of pursuing knowledge for the purposes of gaining control of our world without attending to the deeper, soulful way of knowing would open the way for a more balanced approach to education, one that would bring the spiritual and the intellectual together.

Second, we need to move away from the situation where one way of knowledge is pursued and the other way is muted, dismissed, or tolerated. Right now, the way of knowledge as power, with its focus on disconnected rationalism and subject specialization, as well as the machine metaphor for human life, have the upper hand within Canadian education. While this focus needs to change it would be just as wrong and ill advised to champion the spiritual way of education and to dismiss the importance of the intellectual path. Both ways are needed. To continue to use a body metaphor, we need to breathe with both lungs so as to be healthy. In order to achieve this balance, we need to set the two ways of knowing in a dialogical framework. The intellectual and the spiritual must be brought together into a conversation, much like two friends talking. The focus of this conversation must be on what will enhance the life of the soul, experienced individually and collectively. Through the give and take of the conversation, an intimacy and a harmony will emerge, for if both ways are respected and listened to, they will yield their best for the good of the soul.

Thirdly, I think we need to recognize the important windows to knowledge which suffering, loss, and failure bring and allow these windows to have a place within education. We do an excellent job celebrating success in education. Witness the award ceremonies, graduations, and sports banquets. Much of our present educational practice has been to focus on excellence and to reward those who excel. We have a difficult time with honoring our failures, despite the fact that failure is part of what it means to be human. We do not recognize that sometimes failing a lesson or a course can be an important learning experience.

I remember a time when I was leaving my first school and moving to another city to take up a full-time chaplain position. One of the guidance counselors came and told me that he heard from one of my former students that I was the best teacher she ever had. I protested, "But, she failed my course. Twice!" To which he responded, "Well, I guess she learned a good lesson from that." Obviously, the student had taken to heart not only some of the content of the course I taught but also the way it was taught. This conversation was a good reminder to me that we learn from our failures as much as our successes.

We do not celebrate well enough our simple participation in sports, arts, or service to others. We do not celebrate those students for whom coming though the door each morning is a success in itself. Rather, we focus on the winners and their achievements as most important. We do not often know how to accept the reality of suffering, loss, and death as a part of the human journey through life. At best, we leave the integration and meaning making of these realities to religious meaning makers. We shy away from them. From my many years of chaplaincy experience, I know how significant the death of a colleague, a student or a parent can be on students, staff, and the school community. We know the impact that a natural disaster, like the Ice Storm in Ontario in 1999 or the floods in Quebec and Manitoba, can have upon a community. Failure, loss, and suffering can break through the myth of being in control and show us the limits of our power. Indeed, the realities of suffering, loss, and failure can open us up to the spiritual way of knowing for they can force us to pay attention to the other dimensions of life that hold meaning for us, the dimensions of relationships, connection, love, and life itself.

These three avenues for bringing the two ways of knowing together (balancing intellectual and spiritual ways of knowing, facilitating dialogue, and opening the windows of suffering, loss and failure) will require that we widen our understanding of education and of schooling. They will require not necessarily more time and resources but rather a more conscious and judicious use of our time and resources. If we see the inclusion of spirituality within education as a worthy part of our formation of Canadian citizens, then the changes will be worth it.

CONCLUSION

Ideally, Canadian education should be about the formation of the whole person who is able to pursue a "good life with and for others in just institutions," if I may borrow this phrase from Paul Ricoeur.[26] Educating for a national civic spirituality serves this goal. It does this by connecting the deeper dimensions of life with the outer demands of active civic engagement. In the wider sense spirituality has social and political implications therefore requiring social and political considerations. Our present fixation on the paradigm of knowledge as power within Canadian education needs to be corrected through the inclusion of the spiritual way of knowing. Including spiritual knowing within Canadian education will, of course, challenge our present championing of the pursuit of power, wealth and prestige which are motivational values presently driving Canadian society.

The task of incorporating spiritual education in Canada meets another challenging set of questions. If spiritual education is to ultimately benefit Canadian society it will require that we explore our understanding of Canadian society itself. If education as power is directly related to a vision of Canada where power, wealth and prestige are upheld as values, can a spiritual approach to education be related to an alternative vision of Canada, one that would uphold other values? In this sense, Canadian spiritual education must be directly connected to the larger social project, which is Canada. It must include the social and political landscape as the horizon of meaning in which we seek to live a spiritual life. It must seek to connect individual Canadians with of the *anima mundi*, the soul of the world. In my view the best way to proceed is to focus on the Canadian soul as one expression of the *anima mundi*. The Canadian soul, as part of the larger world and cosmic soul, becomes then a legitimate location for reflection and a necessary ingredient for spiritual education within Canadian schools. Our Canadian soul is the subject, the content, of our spiritual discipline. Let us reflect now upon this Canadian soul.

NOTES

1. Annie Dillard, *Pilgrim at Tinker Creek* (New York: Harper and Row, Publishers, Inc., 1988), pp. 33–34.

2. Steven Glazer, ed. *The Heart of Learning: Spirituality in Education* (New York, NY: Jeremy P. Tarcher/Putnam Press, 1999).

3. See: Clive Beck, "Education for Spirituality" in *Interchange: A Quarterly Review of Education*, Toronto: OISE Press, Vol. 17, No.2, 1986, pp. 148–156; Nel Noddings, *The Challenge to Care in Schools* (New York: Teachers College Press, 1992), pp. 81–85; Parker Palmer, *To Know As We Are Known: A Spirituality of Education* (San Francisco: Harper and Row, 1983); John P. Miller, *The Contemplative Practitioner: Meditation in Education and the Professions* (Toronto: OISE Press, 1994).

4. The theme of spiritual education permeates Thomas Groome's latest book *Educating For Life: A Spiritual Vision for Every Teacher and Parent* (Allen, Texas: Thomas More Press, 1998). See also Maria Harris, *Teaching and Religious Imagination: An Essay in the Theology of Teaching* (New York: HarperCollins, 1987).

5. Dudley Plunkett, *Secular and Spiritual Values: Grounds for Hope in Education* (London: Routledge Press, 1990).

6. To counter the individualism within education Parker Palmer has argued for the centrality of 'troth' to learning, a concept he uses to express the communal dimension of learning throughout his book in *To Know as We Are Known: A Spirituality of Education* (San Francisco: Harper and Row, Publishers, 1983).

7. Charles Taylor, *The Malaise of Modernity* (Concord, Ontario: Anansi Press, 1991), p. 5.

8. Kieran Egan, *Imagination in Teaching and Learning: The Middle School Years* (London, Ontario: The Althouse Press, 1992), pp. 45–65 and William Hare, *What Makes a Good Teacher* (London, Ontario: The Althouse Press, 1993), pp.147–162.

9. Donald Oliver with Kathleen W. Gershman, *Education, Modernity, and Fractured Meaning: Toward a Process Theory of Teaching and Learning* (Albany, N.Y. SUNY Press, 1989), p. 19.

10. Ibid., pp. 11–31.

11. Jane Jacobs, "Credentialing Versus Educating", chapter three in *Dark Age Ahead* (Toronto: Vintage Canada, 2005), pp. 44–63.

12. Dwight Boyd, "Dominance Concealed through Diversity: Implications of Inadequate Perspectives on Cultural Pluralism" in *Harvard Educational Review*, Vol. 66, No. 3, Fall 1996. p. 27.

13. Thomas Berry, *The Dream of the Earth* (San Francisco: Sierra Club Books, 1990), p. 22.

14. John O'Donoghue, *Anam Cara: A Book of Celtic Wisdom* (New York: HarperCollins, 1997), p. 118.

15. Kenneth, C. Russell, "How Contemplatives Read the World" in *Spiritual Life: A Quarterly of Contemporary Spirituality*, Vol. 33, No. 4. Winter, 1987. p. 196.

16. Sharon Butala, *The Perfection of the Morning: An Apprenticeship in Nature* (Toronto: HarperCollins, 1995), p.55.

17. Ibid., p. 56.

18. Katherine Dyckman and Patrick Carroll, *Inviting the Mystic, Supporting the Prophet: An Introduction to Spiritual Direction* (New York: Paulist Press, 1981), p. 79.

19. Raimundo Panikkar, "The Contemplative Mood: A Challenge to Modernity" in *Cross Currents*, Vol. xxxi, No. 3, Fall 1981. p. 261.

20. Margret Buchmann, "The Careful Vision: How Practical Is Contemplation in Teaching" in *American Journal of Education*. Vol. 98, No. 1, November 1989, p. 47.

21. Thomas Merton, *New Seeds of Contemplation* (London. Burns and Oates, 1967), p. 7.

22. See Clive Beck's call for a greater appreciation for the daily, active dimensions of life in spiritual education in *Better Schools: A Values Perspective* (Great Britain: The Falmer Press, 1990), p. 165.

23. Parker Palmer, *The Active Life: Wisdom for Work, Creativity, and Caring* (San Francisco. HarperCollins, 1990), pp. 6–7.

24. Russel Butkus, "Linking Social Analysis With Curriculum Development: Insights From Paulo Freire" in the *Journal of Religious Education*, Vol. 84, No. 4, Fall 1989, p. 572. He argues that the heart of religious education is to promote self development and prophetic communities oriented towards justice. Also, Sandra Bosacki has argued that we need to focus equally on the needs of the individual and the community in "Theory of Mind and Education: Towards a Dialogical Curriculum" in *Holistic Educational Review*. Vol. 10, No. 3, Autumn 1997, pp. 35–38. Finally, Anne Carr has called the drive to integrate a committed work for justice and a deepening of personal interiority a mystical-political spirituality. See Anne Carr, *A Search for Wisdom and Spirit: Thomas Merton's Theology of the Self* (Notre Dame, Indiana: University of Notre Dame Press, 1988).

25. Robert McAfee Brown, *Spirituality and Liberation: Overcoming the Great Fallacy* (Louisville, Kentucky: The Westminster Press, 1988), p. 121.

26. Paul Ricoeur, *Oneself as Another,* trans. Kathleen Blamey (Chicago and London: The University of Chicago Press, 1992).

Chapter Three

Canadian Soul

Patriotism is identification with others in the ongoing life of a political community. The patriot is someone who looks ahead into a future where she hopes her community will persist and prosper, and also behind into the past of her people, a past which, by virtue of identification with her fellow citizens, becomes integral to her own story as well.[1]

I am a fortunate man in many ways because I grew up with a father who instilled in me a love of Canada. One of the favourite pastimes in our home as I grew up was to sit and talk about politics after the evening meal was done. Both my parents have a strong love for this country. Such a love stems from their immigrant roots; it also stems from their personal experience. My father was a member of the Canadian Air Force in which he proudly served for over twenty years. As a young couple, in their mid-twenties and already with three young boys to care for, they were posted to France as part of Canada's commitment to NATO's post-World War II peacekeeping mission at the border between France and Germany. We lived there for three years.

Those three years were a great time for my parents, and they have often spoken of it fondly. They also spoke fondly of their appreciation of Canada upon their return. There was, and continues to be, much to give thanks for in Canada. The standard of living, the social programs, the geography, and the economic opportunities were appreciated in a deeper way while my parents were posted overseas. Upon their return to Canada, they felt a deep sense of gratitude for our country. Indeed, their sense of gratitude was the backdrop for the political conversations that we would have around the table. As a family we would discuss and argue the various merits and demerits of particular political issues or parties. As we grew older the conversations continued, our appreciation for complexity added to our nuances, and our passion for the country continued to grow.

At the head of these table debates about Canada sat my father who was just as opinionated as the rest of us. He encouraged us to think of ourselves as Canadians, to consider the less fortunate, and to show respect for those with whom we disagreed. Much of my passion for the soul of Canada was nurtured around that table. As I reflect upon it all now, I think that we all need places in which we can discuss and debate the soul of our country. Without safe places for political discourse our public life diminishes. It is for this reason that I believe that we need to provide room for the social and the political within our education systems and that we need to see both as part of our civic spirituality. In a sense, educating for a socially and politically responsive civic spirituality is a civic responsibility.

The pioneers and dreamers who gave birth to Canada understood this responsibility and believed in providing an education that promoted a unified vision of Canada, one that would bring different regions together and one that would encourage citizens to work for the common good. They also understood the importance of providing an education that would impart the tools and attitudes required to resist the pressures for assimilation that came from the United States and yet to remain distinct from the European culture. They appreciated the challenges of providing such an education given the vast expanse of land and the diverse regions that were part of our nation.

Today, there is a similar need to identify and pursue a more unified approach to education in light of the challenges and opportunities that face us as a people, as Canada is maturing beyond its bicultural and Judeo-Christian democratic foundations and becoming a multicultural and religiously pluralistic country within a secular democracy. This development is taking place along side the continual search to maintain our distinctive national character in North America while resisting the homogenizing influence of the United States. A key component to such a unified approach is spirituality. There is something providential in the emergence of a respect for spirituality in our secular times. As we begin to recognize the legitimacy of the spiritual way of knowing as harmonious with the rational and scientific way of knowing, we begin to see that including spiritual education within Canadian education is not only a wise pedagogical decision, but also a wise political decision. The connection between the political concerns of nationhood and the spirit of a citizenry is strong and provides fertile ground for education in civic spirituality. Many of the issues that face us as Canadians, from environmental devastation to urban poverty, require an approach that is ultimately rooted in our spirituality.

There are many educational organizations, teacher-led initiatives, and educational programs seeking to address the various issues we face in positive ways. Many of these initiatives are making great strides to contribute to the common good. Yet, these initiatives, while sometimes presuming a spiritual genesis or grounding, do not necessarily explicitly recognize and promote spirituality as a way of knowing. On top of these considerations is the fact that these diverse initiatives are often isolated and lacking in interconnectedness. The result is that their combined potential is lost. This loss of potential is due also to the fact that a coherent approach to spiritual education is lacking across our various locations of education. It is for this reason that I believe that we need to highlight spiritual education across Canada, in all its personal and socio-political ramifications, so as to bring together the many forces for good. Embracing and promoting a civic and national spirituality would serve the Canadian project well.

Educating for a civil spirituality would require an education for soul, in particular, an education that highlights the Canadian soul. Every nation has soul, a way of expressing the *animus mundi* and each way is distinct. In order to educate for our Canadian soul we need to find new language and new points of references for which to engage in a discourse that will satisfy both religious and secular educators. Such points of references would be rooted in our history, be living in our nation today, and provide direction for our future. We need to refer to our core experiences and foundational images and seek out how we give expression to the spiritual way of knowing. In this chapter my concern is with the content of our civic spirituality, the Canadian soul. One image or metaphor that I think captures the notion of the soul is that of the wind.

If there is one force of nature that I have experienced across Canada that has had the ability to constantly draw my attention, it is the wind. No matter where I have been across Canada, from Happy Valley-Goose Bay, Labrador to Waupoos Island off of Prince Edward County in Ontario to Portage Avenue in Winnipeg, Manitoba to Lac La Biche in Alberta to Coppermine, Northwest Territories to the top of the Squamish Chief in British Columbia, I am amazed at the various expressions of the wind in Canada. At times, the wind can be as gentle as a soft kiss on the cheek, bringing with it the slight scent of a late summer harvest or the sweetness of spring flowers. At other times, it can be like a furnace blast carrying hot summer heat across the prairies or the cruel carrier of the Arctic cold that can cut to the bone. No matter how intense or subtle, no matter which direction it hails from, the wind is a bearer of life. It carries the precipitation so necessary for our crops. It helps to pollinate our flowers and to shape our land. It also helps to shape our imagination as a people. The wind is omnipresent. It arrives upon our shores from across the seas, from the north and from the south. It carries with it all that it has picked up along the way before it reaches our land, and then adds all it brings to the texture of our country. Our own landscape, our mountains, our prairies, our hills, our rivers and our lakes, channel the ebb and flow of the wind, affecting its course and the impact. We breathe in this wind with each breath we take, inhaling the gift of life that comes with the wind. The wind continually calls us to pay attention to life.

Whenever I have stood and watched the wind blow, I've experienced a deep love and appreciation for nature. There is nothing like the sound of the wind rustling through the leaves of autumn trees, or howling across a lake to cause one to pause and to listen. To feel the wind upon the face, warm, cold or hot, is to feel the presence of soul. The wind holds both benign and malevolent potential. It gives life and sometimes it takes life away. Storms that ravish our lakes, rivers and seas; twisters and tornadoes that rip through our communities; and rainstorms and snowstorms that rise and fall with the seasons, all point to the power of the wind to wreak havoc. The famed wreck of the Edmond Fitzgerald is one such example of nature's power. Indeed, the wind is a powerful presence and a mighty force.

The wind is an apt metaphor for the soul. If the soul is the animating energy and presence that permeates all of life, it is easy to see how the wind is a natural metaphor of the soul and a reminder of its energy and presence. Like the wind, the soul cannot be seen but we can feel its effects when it passes and when it is absent. Like the wind, the soul can be peaceful and tranquil and give life. It can also be a turbulent threat to life. The absence of wind can provide a stillness that beckons one to listen deeply to the moment. The presence of wind can signal the direction of the life force that beckons us. The wind affects us all. So too does our soul impact upon us as a community and a nation.

The wind is an apt metaphor for the Canadian national soul. It speaks to the presence of the world soul as it flows across Canada. We are not immune to global realities and so as the wind from afar impacts upon our land so too does the *anima mundi* impact upon our national soul. Yet, the wind gains a particular quality as it passes over our land. Thus, the *anima mundi* finds itself refracted through the presence of the Canadian soul, allowing the special characteristics of Canada to be enlivened and spread across our country. Just as the wind, transparent and from away, is known in the local context, so too the soul is transparent and comes from away but is known in how it is felt in our Canadian context. Just as the wind can cause tranquility or turbulence, so too can the soul bring tranquility or turbulence. The bringing together of the soul of the world and the soul of Canada, like the merging of world wind and the Canadian winds, lends itself to a way of seeing the soul across our land, a way that is marked by seeing the transcendent in the immanent and the immanent in the transcendent. The soul is like the wind, it moves where it will. We are wise to watch for it and learn from its teachings.

Is there such a thing as a Canadian soul that blows across our land? To help us answer this question, let us turn to Professor John P. Miller from the Ontario Institute for Studies in Education at the University of Toronto who has been a leader in promoting spirituality and holism within education. In his book *Education and the Soul*, Miller discusses how various world religions and philosophies agree that the concept of the soul refers to the animating energy that guides the created world. He builds upon these traditional understandings of the soul and proposes that the soul has four aspects. First, the soul is an animating energy or process, and in particular, a loving energy. Second, the soul is the seat of our deepest longings and feelings, which we seek to find and to live throughout our life. Third, the soul seeks love and union with other souls through a sense of community. Fourth, the soul lives with paradox and is comfortable with darkness.[2] The soul contains these four elements and yet is not contained by these elements for it remains an elusive and mysterious presence, a presence that moves us into life.

The soul is much more than private and personal. It is also social and communal. Miller quotes Robert Sardello as a person who is concerned about the relationship between the individual soul and the world soul.

> The circulating force or power I shall call soul, and to make clear that what I am calling soul has little to do with individual life alone, by soul I shall always imply the soul of the world as a way of referring to the inseparable conjunction of individual and world; further, this is always a conjunction in depth.[3]

Therefore, just as there is a soul in every person, there is a soul in the world. We generally find this insight very easy to affirm whenever we are out in nature and surrounded by the sights, sounds, and smells of the natural world. Sharon Butala in her autobiographical reflection, *The Perfection of the Morning*,[4] is an example of a Canadian writer who found her vocation as a writer by learning to attend to the presence of the soul as it was manifest in nature.

Jean Vanier, son of the late Governor General Georges Vanier and founder of the worldwide organization of L'Arche that serves mentally disabled adults, has written eloquently about the presence of this greater dimension of ourselves to which we belong.

> We are all part of something greater than ourselves. We all flow from a source that is unfathomable and we are all journeying towards it, carrying with us the

light of truth and love. Each of us is called to be in communion with the source and heart of the universe. The infinite yearnings of our hearts are calling us to be in communion with the Infinite. None of us can be satisfied with the limited and the finite.[5]

The yearning, deep within each of us, to belong and to contribute is a signal of the presence of soul in us and in our surroundings. Soul is found in all of life, in the natural world and in human cultures.

The affirmation of the presence of soul in the realities of human culture and urban civilization may be slightly more difficult to notice than in the natural world and within rural cultures, but it is not impossible. Today, we find the most complex expression of human cultures and civilization in the density of urban life. It can be difficult to experience the soul in the city. Still, when one pays close attention to the life and rhythm of a city, one gradually becomes aware that the sights and the sounds of the people, buildings, roads, and myriads of signs point to the presence of an animating energy. Another location of the soul in the city occurs when diverse cultures interact in festive fashion giving rise to vibrancy in urban culture that is quite distinct from rural or agrarian cultures. The synergy and rhythm of energy that pulse through a city give voice to the presence of soul as it is lived through the creation of human consciousness and longing for connection and meaning. From the experiential knowledge of the soul present in the individual, in the natural world, in the city, in human culture and in civilization itself, the next logical step is to be able to see that every nation has a soul. We can more easily acknowledge the presence of a national soul when we see it present in the lives of individuals and in the collective expressions of the soul that give rise to the flourishing of life in all its goodness, complexity and beauty.

The national soul moves us beyond the personal soul to the communal or collective soul present within a political entity. A national soul is the animating energy, often expressed through the founding myths, symbols, and stories of the nation that flows across the nation animating the citizens of the nation and summoning them to participatory action. A national soul gives voice to the deepest aspirations of its citizens. It is the source of solidarity between individuals within the nation. In addition to exhibiting these attributes, a national soul allows the peoples of the nation to live with paradox, incompleteness, and tragedies because the soul encompasses tranquility and turbulence, light, and shadow. Any people, any nation, can have soul. It is that which adds life, distinctive character and creativity to its citizens and sets it apart from other peoples or nations. The diversity of national souls pulsing through our world today gives expression to the world soul that flows like the wind around our world.

There are some who resist the notion of the *anima mundi* or world soul and who will therefore find it difficult to accept the notion of a national soul. Such resistance is often rooted in a rejection of the universalism implied in the idea of soul, a resistance that has arisen in our time in reaction to ample historical evidence of oppressive actions by those who make universal claims. One might dismiss the existence of a national soul because of concerns about the negative extreme of nationalism, which often feed xenophobia, intolerance, and imperialism. These concerns are not to be easily dismissed. However, I do believe that we can begin to move towards the universal provided we do so from the local context. We move towards the universal via the door of the particular culture. We come to see the *anima mundi* through the collection of national souls that work together in harmony. Such a building up from below, as opposed to imposing from above, lends to a sense of transversalism rather than universalism.[6] Moreover, the concept of soul is more philosophical and psychological than it is ideological and I think it allows for a more nuanced appreciation of collective life than does nationalism, which is often heavily laden with political meanings. Finally, the notion of a national soul that I am suggesting is much more than the simply personal soul advocated by some religious persons who often err on the side of manipulation of the individual for religious reasons. Thus, our personal soul is connected to the national soul, which is connected to the world soul, which is connected to the cosmic soul. These various dimensions of the soul interact. If we say that a person is soulful, we are saying that they live with the awareness of the animating principle of life that resides within them and in their culture, nation, world, and cosmos.

While there are differences between an individual soul and a national soul, they are certainly connected. A national soul provides the context for the emergence and development of the individual soul. Seen in this way, the group soul and the individual soul are not at odds but are related in mutual beneficence. When we apply this mutual beneficence to our spiritual life we see that the more one listens and lives from one's personal soul the more one is able to contribute to the presence of soul in the world, thus adding to the national soul. Likewise, the more we accept the reality of a national soul present and flowing across our land the more individuals are free to live in fidelity to their personal experience of soul. A truth of the spiritual way is that the personal soul and the national soul mutually affect each other. When good happens in the soul of the nation it passes into the lives of individuals. Likewise, when good happens to the individual, it flows to the collective soul. The soul of a nation is symbiotically connected to the souls of her citizens. Given this connection, Canadians need to include civic spirituality, which is essentially about educating for a responsible soulfulness, within our different education systems.

DEFINING THE CANADIAN SOUL

Every nation embodies its soul and expresses its spiritual energy differently. We see this diversity across Canadian society. Moreover, within our nation, different groups and cultures manifest their soul in unique ways. Canada's First Nations have their own unique expressions of soul. So too do Canadians who identify themselves as also Québécois, Acadian, European, African, Indo-Canadian, Chinese-Canadian and other dual identities. The reality is that our Canadian soul includes multiple cultural expressions of soul. Canada's soul is much more than a loose alliance of culturally diverse souls. Our Canadian soul is more than the sum of its parts. Our Canadian soul is deeply rooted in our history, in our political structures, and expressed through our laws and national symbols. It flows across this vast land of ours giving us direction and purpose.

As Canadians, we have struggled to recognize and claim our soul. Traditionally, many cultural leaders and literary voices have argued, we are a people who more often recognize our soul by noting how we differ from others. We are not Europeans. We are not Americans. We are a people in between who are birthing a new identity. Moreover, with our growing multiethnic population due to immigration, we recognize that our soul will necessarily include a sense of dual identities as people embrace Canada as a new home while maintaining affection for their country of origin. The experience of letting go of the old in order to embrace a new identity is primal to our Canadian soul.

In the spiritual life, this path of coming to know oneself by going the way in which one is not known, is understood as the apophatic path.[7] On this path, consciousness of identity emerges in recognition of who one is not. Through the not knowing the knowing comes. Thus, by identifying who we are not, we inevitably, over time, come to see who we are. Such is the case for Canadians seeking to know their soul. It is true that we are a young nation and that we have sought to define ourselves as distinct from our neighbours to the south and across the seas. When we look at our history, including both pre and post-European contact, we now have enough lived experience of who we are to be able to give voice to our soul.

Andrew Coyne has argued that a troubling question for Canadians concerns our raison d'être: "All is not well in this country, and at the bottom of most of our national dilemmas is the same unanswered question: not who we are, but why are we?"[8] His argument structures the question of our national identity within a larger field of concern that of the purpose and meaning of our existence. Such questions probe the heart of our search and cause us to reflect. If our national purpose is not the Manifest Destiny of the United States of America or the ruler of the seas of Mother Britain, then what specifically is our purpose for existence as nation? My hunch is that the answer lies within our soul, for the soul gives us our purpose. We need to listen to the soul in order to hear its directions and to know its promptings.

Our national soul is operative today in our daily lives. It provides us not only with our identity but also with the energy and the motive to be. Given the challenging times we live in, it is critical to our future as a nation that we now claim who we are and what it is we are summoned to be as a people.

Just as the wind is given form, shape and direction by the various currents that arise so too our national soul is shaped and directed by various currents that define us as Canadians. These currents, rooted in our history, circulate today and guide us in our journey into the future. There have been times when certain currents have dominated over others. There are also times when they have flowed together to create the soulful energy so necessary for nation building. We may only recognize our soulfulness in one or two of these currents. When they work together over time we see the presence of our soul as Canadians. Other nations may share in certain of these features. However, it is the particular way in which the various features work together within our specific geographical location and history that creates the uniqueness of the Canadian soul.

I wish to offer some personal observations of the distinctive features of our Canadian soul. I have come to see that there are positive, tranquil currents in the Canadian soul that bring us peace and goodness and which we more easily recognize and accept as Canadian. There are also negative, turbulent currents that cause us turmoil and grief. Taken together the tranquil and turbulent currents give our soul its texture and its distinctiveness. Our soul feeds our identity and gives us purpose. I have chosen to identify these currents based on my experiences of living and working, listening and studying, across various parts of this beautiful country of ours. You, dear reader, will have your own impressions of what constitutes the Canadian soul and might add, or subtract, from the descriptions below. That is how it should be for now is the time for Canadians to ponder and discuss the content of our civil spirituality if we are to begin to move into a new time when the *more* is given room to breathe in our public discussions and in our institutions.

i) Rooted in Nature

The most striking current of the Canadian soul is the fact that our soul is deeply rooted in our appreciation of the natural world. Our connection to the natural world pre-dates our contemporary concern with the environment. It is rooted in the histories of our First Nations who, despite their threatened extinction with the arrival of the Europeans, provided a foundation to the Canadian identity. Our First Nations live within and from a sense of communion with the land. The love and communion with the natural climate and the creatures of the land formed a deep bond between our First Nations and the *anima mundi* that flowed across our land prior to the European invasion and the formation of Canada as a nation. They were, and are, the first soul keepers. Many of the settlers and pioneers who came to this land learned over time to share this aboriginal appreciation for nature. Indeed, they learned from First Nations that one needed to live in respectful harmony with nature and the turning of the seasons if one was to survive. An attitude of working in communion with nature rather than against nature was a necessary ingredient of the Canadian soul from the beginning.

The current revival of our First Nations bodes well for Canada. The stronger their voice becomes across our country, stronger too will our appreciation of the natural world become. This revival, coupled with a growing environmental consciousness, which is global as well as local, promises to contribute to a national will to take decisive actions that protect the environment rather than abuse it. In this sense, the future of Canada is intimately connected to the future of our First Nations.

On top of our aboriginal respect for the natural world was the fact of the location of our nation within a northern climate. No matter where you are within this vast land, the reality of winter and snow is a constant reminder that we are a northern people. Our psyche is shaped by this northern exposure.[9] The cold nights, the long winters, the snow, the sense of thriving in it, through it, and with it. No matter where you are, snow impacts upon our consciousness. In Vancouver, the welcomed sight of snow on the Lions overlooking the city signals the arrival of winter in that temperate coastal oasis.

In addition to our northern climate, the vastness of our land shapes us. Unlike some European countries that you can drive across in a matter of hours, it takes a full week to drive across this country. One has to drive from St. John's, Newfoundland to Tofino, B.C. to fully appreciate the length and the breadth of this land. I have often thought that every high school student should have the opportunity to journey across the rambling rolling country side of the Maritimes and the rugged terrain of Quebec and Ontario; see Niagara Falls and the Great Lakes and the land north of the Superior; cross the endless prairies and continue to the foothills on the edge of Calgary; wind their way through the Rocky Mountains to the Coastal Mountains until they reach the Pacific; or fly north to Churchill, Whitehorse, Yellowknife, or Labrador City where they would see that vast expanse of land speckled with lakes and rivers, covered with muskeg and tundra. Then they would know, in their bones, the grandeur of our territories for each region offers its own natural beauty and its own challenges. The harsh yet beautiful texture of our land-scape reaches deep within the Canadian soul and deepens the longer you live upon this land making it one of the essential currents of the Canadian soul.

Canadians have a strong attachment to our vast land and possess an almost symbiotic relationship with the climate. Perhaps both explain why we value our national, provincial, and municipal parks so much. We can understand then how ecological sustainability and environmental activism would find a receptive audience amongst Canadians for we know that our lives are inti-mately connected to the land and to our climate. It is because of our intimacy with nature that we have such prophetic voices as David Suzuki and that Greenpeace was founded here. Our love of nature, folded within our con-sciousness within our northern climate, which our First Nations have known intuitively and experientially, has emerged as a defining feature of the Cana-dian soul. We are at our best when we live in congruence with this part of our soul and, quite frankly, we suffer immensely when we ignore it.

ii) Inclusion

A second current of Canadian soul is our inclusiveness. Canadians are gener-ally hospitable people and open to the new, whether it is in the field of ideas or in our relationships. We generally welcome strangers, turning them into honored guests. Was this not what happened when Maritimers opened their communities to the thousands of Americans who were forced to land on Ca-nadian soil on September 11th, 2001? Is this not the attitude that allowed us to welcome new immigrants at different times during our history? Is it not our openness that leads us to entertain new ideas, sifting them through our collec-tive lens and incorporating them into our social matrix making Canada on a truly progressive country? Indeed, our inclusiveness of the *other*, whether the *other* is the newcomer or a new idea, is part of our collective soul.

When we look at our history, we can see our capacity for openness in our immigrant roots and our preference for cultural and religious integration rather than assimilation. From the long arc of Canadian history we know that we are all, except of course for our aboriginal sisters and brothers, as Newfoundlanders say, "from away". That is, we are all immigrants to this country. We may, as was the case with my ancestors, have immigrated to this land generations ago as explorers, traders and settlers. We may have immigrated shortly after the world wars. We may have immigrated just this week. Regardless of when we arrived, we carry with us the sense that we are an immigrant nation, a nation whose consciousness is directly connected to being newcomers in a foreign land. The experience of being welcomed into a new place where we are invited to establish a home is often reciprocated later in our openness and welcome of others who seek to make Canada their home.

There has always been a struggle between two very different historical forces seeking to shape this current of the Canadian soul, the force for assimilation and the force of integration. Ever since Lord Durham famously advocated for the assimilation of the French within English Canada there has been a deep and long lasting resistance to cultural assimilation within the Canadian psyche. Assimilation is very different from integration. When a people are assimilated, their identity is subsumed within the predominant culture and is lost. The loss of their cultural identity is what Francophone Canadians have resisted and continue to resist. Much of Quebec nationalism of today is rooted in resentment due to pressures to favor cultural assimilation imposed by English Canada. This resistance gave rise to a sense of two solitudes within Canada. The historical experience of two solitudes and the coexistence of two different cultures laid the framework for the emergence of our multicultural society today. It is hard to think that Canadian multiculturalism, despite its limitations and its challenges, would have found such a receptive field had not the French resisted assimilation throughout our history. Indeed, the Québécois resistance to assimilation within an Anglophone hegemony laid the foundation for present day multiculturalism.

Our Canadian practice has been to favour integration rather than assimilation. With integration, a culture can belong to a larger collective culture without losing its particular cultural identity. Integration means to "come into equal membership of society, without regard for race or religion."[10] Distinct cultures and races are able to achieve equal membership in the larger Canadian society. This equal membership is achieved by focusing on what the different cultures hold in common, eliminating any barriers to equality between cultures, and valuing differences in such a way that the unifying bond is enriched rather than diminished. Many cultures within Canada have shared the Québécois resistance to assimilation. People from Europe, Asia, Latin America, and Africa have all, with varying degrees of success, resisted the loss of their cultural identities within Canada. Indeed, the Canadian experience, which we proudly proclaim, is one of a cultural mosaic, a tapestry, rather than the melting pot vision of our neighbours to the direct south of us.

The resistance to assimilation gave rise to the promotion of multiculturalism. Granted it has not always been easily obtained, and there has been resistance to ethnic minorities throughout our history. There have been many successes along the way, perhaps the most noteworthy being the Canadian Charter of Rights and Freedoms, which guarantees that every Canadian citizen be treated equally regardless of their differences. This success has been significant, and while there are many issues still to be resolved, we can see how the Canadian soul's propensity towards openness has given rise to a nation where integration and multiculturalism are considered key ingredients of Canadian identity.

iii) Justice

Another notable current of our Canadian soul is the high esteem that we bestow upon the pursuit of a just society. Our appreciation of justice is one that has emerged over our experience with nation building. The centrality of justice to the Canadian soul is similar to the centrality of freedom to the soul of the United States. The Canadian ideal of justice is deeply rooted in the religious communitarian philosophies that have influenced the formation of Canada from the beginning. The core insight of communitarian philosophy is that a human being becomes a person *vis-à-vis* the community. The community provides the context for the flourishing of the person. There are limits to this communitarian philosophy, one of which is the tendency to suppress creativity in individuals. Nonetheless, the Canadian notion of justice finds one of its roots within the religious, communitarian notion of justice.

Justice within the communitarian view is not necessarily based on the liberal idea of the rights of autonomous individuals but more so on the equality of persons in community. The notion of the equality of persons holds that human persons are intrinsically worthy of respect but that each person is different. In a communitarian worldview justice is understood as fairness rather than right. Justice as fairness requires that consideration be given to the differences between persons and distributed according to capacity and need. This communitarian notion of justice as fairness finds a distinct expression in the concept of redistributive justice, a concept that historically informed many of our Canadian convictions regarding the economy and care of the weak. The communitarian notion of justice as fairness helped to give birth to our lauded social programs, from pensions, to health care, to welfare. Deep within the communitarian philosophy of justice is a sense of duty to care for others and it is the motivation to care for the community that animates the movements for social justice.

Still, as Canada moved into the secular age, the communitarian understanding of justice has been increasingly contested within Canada by the libertarian view of justice. It was John Rawls, in his *A Theory of Justice*,[11] who articulated justice as based on the principle of contract and individual rights. In this view, justice is achieved by balancing the rights of rational beings who agree to exchange goods and services for mutual benefit. There is a fine balance in society then to promote and maintain this mutuality of benefit. This principle of justice is invoked whenever there is a violation of this mutuality and equality, whenever someone is harmed. Canadians have a deep and acute sense of justice. We desire the conditions for all people to be able to pursue the good life and anything that impedes or interferes with that pursuit is to be prohibited in law and custom.

The growth of this libertarian, contractual view of justice within Canada has certainly accelerated since the passage of the Canadian Charter of Rights and Freedoms in which people are to be treated equality regardless of race, religion, gender, sex, language, ability, and sexual orientation. In our time, we are witnessing the social and political preference for the contractual rather than the communal view of justice. Still, at times these two roots of justice, the communitarian and the libertarian, come into conflict in the public sphere especially when we get into the areas of sexual and procreative ethics. We saw this with the recent divisive and charged debate around legalizing same-sex marriage in Canada. Here we saw a clash of the communitarian notion of justice, which permits different treatment of citizens based on their differences, and the liberal notion of justice as a contractual right, which refuses to discriminate between people based on differences. Many who opposed the legalization of same-sex marriage did so on the grounds that it violated tradition communal understandings of the procreative goal of marriage. They often appeal to a biological interpretation of natural law theory as their rationale. Many who favored the legalization of same-sex marriage did so on grounds of human rights, which were inalienable to citizenship and if inalienable could not, therefore, be denied to any citizen based on gender, sex, or sexual orientation. This debate tested these two differing views of justice, straining the Canadian soul in the midst of the debate.

The tension between communitarian and libertarian views on justice feeds this current of the Canadian soul. Indeed, it seems that our Canadian soul expresses its notion of justice not only through the communitarian view of justice as fairness but also through the libertarian view of justice as a contractual right. Somehow, we have been able to achieve a balance in the holding of these two different approaches so that the core virtue of justice is upheld as a core operational value for Canadian society. Perhaps it is due to a Canadian propensity to be able to look at life through a more inclusive *both/and* lens rather than an exclusive *either/or* lens. Regardless of the reason, the pursuit of justice within our society is a testimony to the tenacity of the Canadian soul in that it is able to embrace such divisive debates until an acceptable approach to justice is reached.

iv) Compassion

A fourth current of the Canadian soul, intimately linked to justice, is that of compassion. This current is deeply rooted in our history. The first Canadian settlers (or invaders, depending upon your perspective) would not have survived the first cold, brutal winters in this land if it were not for the fact that the aboriginals bestowed compassion upon them. This notion of being compassionate towards one's neighbours is deeply connected to our land and our climate. From neighbours helping neighbours in order to survive till the next harvest, to the sharing of food during the Great Depression, to the food banks today and to the multitude of community fundraising initiatives that exist across the land, we see the efforts of ordinary citizens to help out their neighbours in need. Our compassion, when wedded to the current of justice, led to the creation of our lauded social safety net. It is rooted in our Judeo-Christian heritage in which the care of others was sustained through various church organizations and programs. These continue today within the growing diversity of religious organizations that exist in our land. For example, I am reminded of the Multifaith Housing Initiative in Ottawa, a non-profit multifaith organization founded to increase housing options for poor and low-income residents of Ottawa. This organization is a prime example of how our different religions are working together to show compassion and caring for society's marginalized.

Our compassionate impulse was also carried forth into our foreign policies, which have been strongly marked by a humanitarian thrust. Our involvement in NATO was often due to the sense of being part of the post-WWII rebuilding of Europe. Lester B. Pearson won the Nobel Peace Prize for his contribution to the resolution of the Suez Canal Crisis and his idea of the creation of a peacekeeping force to be of service to the world. We see further evidence of our compassion in our presence of the world stage in the proliferation of Canadian non-government organizations serving humanitarian goals worldwide, in the growth of the volunteer sector, and in the number of non-profit organizations addressing multiple community needs.

Compassion is a salient current of the Canadian soul, one rooted in our history and in our present realities. Moreover, partly due to the growing influence of Buddhism and aboriginal spirituality we see today our compassion being extended to include all sentient beings and the natural world. Such a widening of our compassion feeds our environmentalism. Compassion, rooted in our hearts' ability to walk with the other in their time of need, is a strength, which we as Canadians have. It helps to temper our reflection on how we should be it the world, providing for a more humane response to difficult situations.

v) Compromise

The final current of the Canadian soul is our appreciation of the need to compromise in order to sustain the common good. This ability to compromise does not mean that we do not hold strong positions. Quite the contrary, we can be very clear and principled in our differences. Perhaps due to the vastness of our land and our living in a challenging climate, we recognize that in order to survive we need to seek the middle path whenever possible. It is a testimony to the health of our democracy for democracy is the practice of the middle way in politics. Indeed, democracy can sometimes be a messy political process. Nonetheless, democracy, as the exercise of public reasoning, provides the political framework for the progressive pursuit of justice and the common good.[12] Canadian democracy provides the open place to arrive at middle positions on matters of common concern and the Canadian values of justice, compassion and inclusion are brought to bear on public policy. We know that we often have to compromise in order to achieve a larger, common good. Indeed, the notion of the common good is a background philosophical framework that informs our political consciousness.

The Canadian ability to compromise is another defining current of the Canadian soul that flows across our country. It enables us to embark upon a venture into the future with a pilgrim mentality and with an understanding that we are on a journey. It serves our openness to the new and fuels a sense of wonder. It roots our optimism and our vitality as a people.

This ability to compromise is closely aligned with one of the main characteristics of spiritual growth, the ability to live with ambiguity. The spiritual path is never a straight path of clear answers, but rather a meandering path through the various exigencies that face us as we journey. To be able to live with ambiguity then points to a largesse in our soul, that we are able to hold the seemingly incommensurable factors of life together for the common good. There is plenty of evidence throughout our history that we as a people are able to live with ambiguity and that we express this through our willingness to compromise when necessary for the common good. The recent decision regarding the legalization of same-sex marriages is an example of our ability to live with ambiguity in order to support the common good. This decision does not sit well with some Canadians. Nonetheless, all Canadians are bound to respect the law that permits this reality. It is through such compromises and through the embrace of ambiguity that our national soul is shaped.

Living attuned to the natural world, being inclusive, valuing justice, being compassionate and embracing compromise are recognizable currents of the Canadian soul. These currents are rooted in our history as a people, and flow across our country today. These currents are present in greater and lesser degrees throughout different points of our history and across the various regions of our vast land. Taken together, they point to the ways in which the soul of our country is alive and how our soul can be discerned. They flow in the background of our public discourse about our country and through the parts of our identity that we continually struggle to express through our national project.

Some might argue that other nations reveal these same features. What makes our living of these features so unique is the fact that we do so as a people with a relatively sparse population spread across a vast land mass in a northern climate. The fact that we have given voice to the value of the natural world, to inclusion, to justice, to compassion, and to compromise in the face of the limitations found in our small population in our vast land is a testimony to the strength and vibrancy of the Canadian soul. These features are embedded in our history, our symbols, and our laws. From across our great landscape and within our northern climate, our soul gives shape to our identity and our purpose as Canadians.

This list is not exhaustive and you will have your own insights to add to what constitutes our Canadian soul and this is as it should be. The soul of a nation is never fixed, it is constantly evolving, adapting, and changing. The important thing is to take part in the conversation and to educate for the Canadian soul in everyday life. It is important to take part in conversations about what it is that makes us Canadians and why we exist as a country. The questions and the conversations will lead to clarification and to a deepening of identity.

TURBULENCE IN CANADIAN SOUL

While there are tranquil currents in our national soul, which have grown stronger over time and which contribute to our national identity, there are also turbulent currents that tend to undermine our communal life. These are areas that have just as much power to influence our national psyche as the tranquil currents of our soul but which, if unacknowledged or repressed, can cause havoc. Indeed, as the insightful psychologist Carl Jung argued much of our spiritual life is unconscious and held within the shadow of our life.

> The shadow is composed for the most part of repressed desires and uncivilized impulses, morally inferior motives, childish fantasies and resentments, etc.—all those things about oneself one is not proud of... To the degree that we identify with a bright persona, the shadow is correspondingly dark... The shadow is not, however, only the dark underside of the personality. It also consists of instincts, abilities, and positive moral qualities that have long been buried or never been conscious.[13]

As Jung theorized, the shadow is that area of our soul where our repressed desires, instincts, and fantasies live. If not acknowledged, these fantasies play out in our conscious life, sometimes in uncontrollable ways, more often in the distortion of our authentic self. We see it happen in our personal life particularly in our personal relationships. We can also see it happen within our collective and national life. There, repression can lead to the distortion or rejection of common values that serve a people thereby contributing to social decline.[14] Indeed, an unrecognized shadow operating within our national soul can have serious consequences for us as a people and cause substantial turbulence for our nation.

We recognize our collective shadow when our currents are distorted and disturbed, wreaking havoc in the same way as do windstorms, twisters, or tornadoes when they pass. Thus, while our Canadian soul is aligned with our close proximity to nature, we have to admit that we have not always respected the natural environment. Indeed, given our consumer lifestyle and our resource-based economy we as Canadians are implicated in the reality of environmental desecration. We *are* major polluters. The pollution of our Great Lakes, the smog in our cities, the collapse of our resource industries (fisheries and forestry, in particular), all point to our irresponsible stewardship of our natural world. Moreover, the tardiness of our response to climate change and our resistance in recent years to legislation that would protect the environment point to the presence of this turbulent current in our national soul, one that is disconnected from our natural world. Our deep and systemic resistance to changing our lifestyles and acting politically, so that the environment can recover, point to the reality that we are not yet living congruently with our conscious awareness for action.

When we turn to the current of the Canadian soul experienced as openness towards others and the welcoming of different cultures, we see the presence of turbulence as well. There is plenty of evidence of racism, discrimination, and the persistence of colonial mentalities simmering just below the surface of our society. Our First Nations, through their experience of being relegated to reservations and through their experience of the residential school system, are a poignant reminder of systemic racism within Canada. While there have been moments when redress and reconciliation have occurred, our political history has been one of persistent refusal to treat our First Nations as equal partners in our nation. Elsewhere, the attempt to force the assimilation of the French within an English country and the expulsion of the Acadians are examples of times when assimilation seem to win over integration. The treatment of Canadians of Japanese and Chinese ancestry during the Second World War as well as our turning our backs upon the needs of Jews during that same war are further evidence of latent racism and religious intolerance.

Racial and cultural enclaves remain within Canada today: some chosen and some imposed. The truth is, that despite our propensity to openness there are plenty of examples of systemic discrimination, racism, and religious persecution, proof of our closed mindedness and lack of hospitality. Indeed, from the lack of women in positions of leadership, to the evidence of discrimination based on country of origin, to the longstanding resistance to settling the legitimate claims of our First Nations, there are many places within our national history and in our current practices in which we can see that a negative side of our national soul is still at work, one that undermines our openness.

We see the turbulence in our soul's quest for justice in our lack of fairness, our blatant disregard for the needs of others, our exclusionary practices, and our unequal treatment of citizens based on race, gender, religion, culture, or sexual orientation; a treatment which is prohibited under our Charter. We have numerous examples of how the turbulence of injustice has found expression in our national history particularly during the period prior to the passage of the Charter. The long battle for equal rights for women is rooted in a systemic injustice that favors patriarchal privilege. This injustice continues today in the court battles for pay equity. There are numerous untold stories, across this land, of people who were denied employment or job promotions because of their linguistic, gender, racial, or religious affiliation. The continuing scandal of the living conditions of many of our First Nations persists despite our best efforts, pointing to a deeper resistance to solution, a resistance located in our soul. Finally, the resistance, in many sectors of Canada, to providing fair and non-discriminating treatment towards homosexuals is a more recent example of this turbulence at play within our national soul. When Pierre Elliot Trudeau gave voice to the notion of Canada as a just society he did so not only because of the potential for justice that lay within our grasp but also because there was ample evidence of injustice throughout our history and across our land that could only be changed by turning our national soul to the value of justice.

The turbulent side of the Canadian capacity for compassion is indifference, apathy, and the lack of empathy. There has always been the presence of this turbulence within us as a people and there have been times when this destructive current has been particularly present. Most recently, we witnessed the absence of compassion during the political struggles of the 1990's. During that decade federal and provincial governments drastically slashed funding for Canada's lauded social safety net in order to eliminate deficit financing and to increase productivity. We also witnessed throughout this time acrimonious public debates regarding the sustainability of our public health care system. The breadth of compassion within Canadian society, often originating from religious convictions, succumbed to fear and protectionism. The result has been a widening of the gap between the rich and the poor in country, the creation of a stressed middle class that has fewer resources to channel towards compassion for the unfortunate, the creation of a "functional underclass"[15] that includes the underemployed, the working poor and the homeless. Our minimal foreign aid commitment, in light of our collective wealth, is further indication of how our compassion is undermined by our fear. The widening of the gap has had serious repercussions for developing countries around the globe. We have plenty of evidence, then, of how and when our national propensity for compassion has been taken over by apathy and indifference towards the weaker members of our community and our global village. This turbulent stream is rooted in our fear and our greed.

For all the evidence of the famous Canadian ability to seek compromise, to tolerate paradox, and to live with uncertainty, there is plenty of evidence of the presence of rigid fundamentalism within our nation. We see this stance on the part of some who believe they possess the only truth. Truth can be religious or secular, philosophical or empirical, cultural, or personal. We often associate such fundamentalism with religion and there is truth to this observation. We can also see fundamentalism within our economic ideology of capitalism, our philosophy of championing rationalism, or our parading of our individual rights over and against the values found in communities. There are many places and communities within our country where people's perspectives are restrained only by the rule of law and its protection of equality and non-discrimination. A more recent example would be the need to place restraints upon some individuals who stridently opposed equality for homosexual persons. Free speech is permitted but not if it violates Canada's anti-hate laws. So, the turbulent strain of ideological fundamentalism is present within the Canadian ability to embrace compromise, paradox, and uncertainty.

These turbulent strains within our national soul, as in our personal soul, have a negative impact if we are not conscious of them. Turbulence possesses a tremendous amount of energy: energy that can be used for good if we consciously channel it, but which will cause considerable damage if it is not respected and consciously channeled. Thus, the energy that goes into maintaining a standard of living that ignores the environment, into closing down ideas and cultures rather than celebrating differences, into continuing unjust practices, into failing to be compassionate, and into maintaining rigid ideological positions, is energy that is not used to build up the common good and the national soul. The learning task is one of recognizing and owning the energy in these turbulent strains so as to promote the common good. We can never eradicate turbulence, but we can move towards greater consciousness of the presence and power of tranquility and turbulence within our national soul.[16] Education for our national soul is the task of our times.

Our Canadian soul, then, is a mixture of tranquil and turbulent energies. Just as the combined features of our tranquil side together reveal our soul, so too does the combination of our turbulent energies reveal our national soul. The soul holds both types of currents and they flow together to give shape to our country. It is full of energy and potential as well as failure and lethargy. It is alive within us, in our laws, in our stories, in our media, in our personalities, in our politics, and in our individual lives.

The Canadian soul is the content of our civic spirituality. Our national soul shapes our identity and gives us our purpose. It is wise then that we include our national soul as part of our education for a civic spirituality. Ultimately, including spirituality within Canadian education will help to magnify a sense of Canadian soulfulness that would benefit all Canadians in the long run. But, how do we go about educating for such national soul? It is to this pedagogical question that we now turn our attention.

NOTES

1. Eamonn Callan, "Pluralism and Civic Education" in *Studies in Philosophy and Education*, Vol. II. 1991, p. 75.

2. John P. Miller, *Education and the Soul: Toward a Spiritual Curriculum* (Albany, NY: SUNY Press, 2000), pp. 24–28.

3. Robert Sardello, *Facing the World with Soul* (Hudson, NY: Lindisfarne Press, 1992), p. 21.

4. Sharon Butala, *The Perfection of the Morning: An Apprenticeship in Nature* (Toronto: HarperCollins, 1994).

5. Jean Vanier, *Becoming Human* (Toronto: Anansi Press, 1998), p. 118.

6. This is a term that some feminists have put forth to counteract the negative impact of universalism without losing the necessity of articulating the whole in the largest sense.

7. William H. Shannon, *Thomas Merton's Dark Path: The Inner Experience of a Contemplative* (New York, NY: Farrar, Straus, Giroux, 1981), pp. 9–12.

8. Andrew Coyne, "All is not well in Canada. Don't shrug." *MacLean's* (April 14th, 2008), p. 40.

9. Mary Jo Leddy, "Theology in the Canadian Context" in *Faith That Transforms: Essays in Honor of Gregory Baum* (New York/Mahwah: Paulist Press, 1987), pp. 127–134.

10. *The Concise Oxford Dictionary of Current English* (Oxford: Oxford University Press, 1976).

11. John Rawls, *A Theory of Justice* (Cambridge: Harvard University Press, 1971).

12. Amartya Sen, "Democracy as Public Reason", Chapter 15 in *The Idea of Justice* (Cambridge, MA: The Belknap Press of Harvard University Press, 2009), pp. 321–337.

13. Daryl Sharpe, *Jung Lexicon: A Primer of Terms & Concepts* (Toronto: Inner City Press, 1991), pp. 123–124.

14. For a discussion on the significance of incorrect judgments and negative bias and their impact upon group consciousness and thought see Bernard Lonergan, *Method in Theology* (New York: Seabury Press, 1972), pp. 36–41.

15. John Kenneth Galbraith, *The Culture of Contentment* (Boston: Houghton Mifflin Company, 1992), pp. 30–41.

16. I am indebted here to Robert A. Johnson for his insights into the positive sides of the shadow and the need for balance in the psychological life. See his *Owning Your Own Shadow: Understanding the Dark Side of the Psyche* (New York, NY: HarperCollins, 1991).

Chapter Four

Engaged Spirituality

We are being carried along by a surge for meaning, which, contrary to many religious beliefs, is not drawing us away from the world but plunging us more profoundly into it, not alienating us from the divine but re-connecting us with the God who co-creates at the heart of creation. Not surprisingly therefore, the new spiritual search takes on global significance for many of its adherents.[1]

I had been serving as chaplain in a suburban high school for several years and took satisfaction in the fact that several of the programs in which I took part were apparently successful. One of these was the annual day of service, in which our graduating students were invited to participate. This event was a day in which these students were encouraged to volunteer their time and talents and to serve people in the larger community. One venue for the service day took place at a small farm just outside the city where a non-profit organization offered holidays and respite experiences for families in need. The farm, like many non-profit projects, ran on a shoestring budget and relied heavily upon volunteerism in order to maintain its programs. Our task for the day was to help in the fall cleanup and to prepare the farm for winter. A crew of about a dozen teens, both male and female, and myself set out by school bus and arrived at the farm around 9:00 a.m. to begin our day of service. We were assigned various tasks, ranging from raking leaves, to painting, to cleaning out the barn and the cottages where the families stayed.

Four from the group were assigned a task that took almost the entire day. They had to move several cords of firewood from the back fields where it had been cut to the basement of the farm house where it would be more eas-ily accessible throughout the winter since it was the fuel to heat the house. The transference meant that the wood had to be placed, piece-by-piece, onto a flatbed and pulled by tractor to the side of the farmhouse, where it was unloaded. Then, each piece of firewood was handed, again piece-by-piece, through a small window leading into the basement wood room in the farm-house. Two students unloaded and passed the wood through the gap created by the window into the basement below to two other students who then stacked the wood neatly in the room. After a short period, the students arrived at a rhythm of heaving and hoeing interspersed with teenage talk, laughter, and song.

On the bus ride home later that afternoon I sat beside one of the young women who had helped move the firewood. She told me that she had a great day and that the experience of moving the firewood was the most spiritual thing she had ever done. When I asked her to explain, she pointed out that she rarely went to church as such yet hadn't dismissed God outright. She just simply didn't put much store in church stuff. She had volunteered for the service day because it made sense to her. She liked to help people and serving at the farm sounded like a neat idea. In moving the firewood she felt good inside and satisfied that her work was adding to the happiness of others.

Her experience of spiritual learning, acquired through a service day demonstrates the importance of engagement as crucial to spiritual education today. Over the years, as more and more schools have embraced service learning or engaged service as part of their overall school programs, we have seen the growth and development of engaged spirituality. Such development is something that needs to be amplified within Canadian education. In order to so amplify, we need to look at the pedagogical concerns of how to educate for spirituality in Canada today. The key is the question of engagement and to this we now turn.

Spiritual education is about turning the soul of the individual to the soul of the world. When contextualized within a particular nation or culture this turning of the soul includes the presence of soul in community, systems, and nations. For Canadian educators spiritual education requires identifying an acceptable method that would serve our nation's soul. Such a method must provide enough consistency and enough flexibility to be responsive the many different regions in which teachers work across this land. More importantly, we need to adopt a method for spiritual education that respects the two streams of education, secular and religious, which currently flow throughout Canada. The young woman who found the spiritual in moving firewood provides a clue to a way that will meet both secular and religious educators. That is, the traditional method of contemplation-in-action, found predominantly in religious but also within non-religious circles, can be rearticulated as engaged spirituality in such a way that the differing needs of both secular and faith based schools can be met and respected. It is a method that can be followed in any location as long as there are teachers open to allowing themselves to be used as guides for turning the souls of their students to the soul of Canada. Here I will offer some of reasons why contemplation-in-action is an appropriate method for Canadian engaged spirituality. In the following chapter, I will develop some strategies that are essential for the teaching of this path.

One of the most encouraging movements within Western education today is the development of pedagogies for spiritual education.[2] Indeed, Parker Palmer[3] and others have argued for the inclusion of spiritual practices within formal education as a corrective to the objectivist, cognitive, and behaviorist agenda presently driving Western education in our global and capitalist age. Such practices include developing the contemplative dimension in teaching; attending to the inner life of teachers and students; teaching various forms of meditation; promoting altruistic service projects and engaged learning; and appreciating religious and non-religious expressions of the sacred. Very often, the horizon of action that encompasses both teachers and learners of spirituality is that of engagement in actions that promote social justice, environmental sustainability, and global citizenship. A common aim in these approaches is to help students develop the tools for personal reflection and to also develop their sense of responsibility for others.

Moreover there is growing, within Western education, a stream of thought that calls for deliberate attention to one's inner personal life simultaneously with the active life of communal and political action. Advocates of this direction hail from religious and non-religious worldviews. We see the concern in such American organizations as the Center for Contemplative Mind in Society; the multifaith contemplative center in Hudson, New York called Garrison Village; and the influential Fetzer Institute in the United States. We see this attention to the integration of inner and outer dimensions of life inside explicitly religious education systems as well. In fact, well-known Catholic educator Thomas Groome from Boston College has promoted such a vision in one of his most recent books.[4] The overarching concern of these thought leaders and these centres of learning is that of connecting the spiritual life with social and political action, particularly if such actions are focused on the environment. Such a stream can rightly be called education for engaged spirituality.

The spiritual has never really been absent from the Canadian experience. Our close affiliation with the natural world has always held the potential to draw us into the spiritual way of knowing. In fact, there are many geographical areas which people have traditionally identified as being locations for the sacred. I remember when I lived in Owen Sound, Ontario hearing that the Bruce Peninsula was considered a geographical place of healing because of its rock grounding in the Canadian shield while be bordered on two sides by beautiful waters, Lake Huron and Georgian Bay. We can also think of many places which our aboriginal brothers and sisters consider sacred, often their burial grounds. For example, Lac St. Anne in Alberta is considered a sacred lake by the First Nations. A few years ago there was an article in the Ottawa citizen that pointed out the spiritual significance of St. Joseph's Oratory in Montreal, a significance that spoke to people from various religious traditions. Indeed, Canada is full of many examples of places where the spiritual is considered important.

There are also several thought leaders who are promoting such a path. I have already mentioned Clive Beck and Jack Miller. In addition to these authors, we have the contribution of Edmund O'Sullivan, one of the leaders of transformative learning in Canada. Indeed, in the epilogue of his book *Transformative Learning,* we find a fine articulation of the need to incorporate spirituality within education today.[5] Then, of course, we have the prophetic leadership of our own David Suzuki who, in *The Sacred Balance,* integrates the spiritual dimension within his ecological ethics.[6] These authors are trying to find new language and new ways of articulating the spiritual life in ways that are appropriate to our present day concerns.

There is something, then, emerging within Canada in which people are recognizing the need to bring together the personal, the social, and the political into an integrated spirituality. Some of these initiatives are new offshoots of traditional religious approaches. Some are new expressions of secular and scientific approaches that are integrating the mystical into their agenda. Regardless of their differing narrative origins these emerging centres, networks, and organizations are making a true and lasting contribution to the fostering of a civil spirituality responsive to our Canadian needs within a global village. Moreover, within the field of education practitioners and theorists are making a significant contribution to the development of a civil and engaged spirituality. Some secular educators, free of the doctrinal concerns and circularity that often inhibits religious educators, are implementing spiritual practices in the hope of unleashing the creative power of the spirit within schools. I note here some steps that some educators within the Vancouver Public School system have taken in order to teach mindfulness. These steps are tentative as practitioners often seek to stay below the radar of public scrutiny because spirituality remains a contentious and disputed concern. Within the field of religious education there is a growing awareness of the need to include education for justice, peace, and sustainability, as constitutive of religious worldviews. Like their secular counterparts, religious educators proceed slowly so as to avoid negative reactions from either stridently religious policy makers or stridently secular scrutinizers.

However encouraging this new field of educational focus is, we need to be mindful that it is still young and has yet to enter the mainstream of educational practice. In order to provide the best possible education for spirituality in Canada, we need to encourage an honest dialogue and synthesis between religious and non-religious approaches. A secularist's openness to the *more* to life and a religious person's openness to the *more* in the present world are necessary preconditions for an honest dialogue to take place. For this dialogue to mature, secularists need to be open to including the insights from religious traditions. Every religious tradition has a font of wisdom concerning the spiritual life that would supplement and compliment the work of secular spiritual educators. Likewise, religious educators need to acknowledge ways in which religious worldviews have sometimes negatively contributed to our contemporary problems. Secular insights into spirituality can add to the wisdom found in religious spiritualities. A dialogue between secular and religious spiritual educators would do wonders to stimulate a civic spirituality in Canada.

In light of the role which faith traditions have played and continue to play in the creation of the Canadian soul and identity, including secular pluralism, I would like to explore how the method of contemplation-in-action, a spiritual method found in most world religions as well as in many humanist philosophies, can provide a foundational method for this new field of engaged spirituality within education. I shall first describe how the historical way of contemplation-in-action is an appropriate method for the promotion of engaged spirituality if we understand it within a framework of social and political action. Then, I shall discuss some of the main insights from engaged spirituality and how these apply to our Canadian context.

CONTEMPLATION-IN-ACTION

Most religions of the world have traditionally upheld that becoming a human person involves the pursuit of both the inner, contemplative and the outer, active dimensions of life. The emphasis is placed upon becoming. The seeds of one's humanity are planted in conception and are nurtured through the life-long engagement and integration of both the inner life of reflection and the outer life of action. The nurturing and growth into authentic and full humanity takes place with, in, and through community. Thus, relationships and community are pre-conditions for personhood. Due to the symbiosis between the personal and the collective, between action and reflection, contemplation in action is a fit method for civil spirituality.

In 1973, there was a unique conference held in Huston, Texas on the topic of contemplation and action. At that conference, representatives from Judaism, Christianity, First Nations, Buddhism, Islam and Sufism met and discussed the traditional approaches to contemplation and action in light of the challenges of our modern world. Despite differences of emphasis and doctrine, a constant in the dialogue was the appreciation for the contemplative attentiveness to the underlying unity in life, acting in accord with this awareness, and the promotion of integration and balance between the two as much as possible.[7] This event was a groundbreaking meeting, one that gave fruit to other such encounters and encouraged dialogue between the various world religions on this shared path of spiritual learning. For example, in 1997 a meeting between Christian and Buddhist monks took place at Gethsemani Trappist Monastery in Kentucky. During this weeklong meeting, the participants shared in meditation and in dialogue, seeking to give voice to where commonality can be found between Christian and Buddhist monasticism.[8] This meeting itself was the fruit of the seeds of newness planted by the famous Trappist monk, Thomas Merton, who through his writings and life sought to open up dialogue between different faith traditions.

It is true that world religions have traditionally concerned themselves with personal and collective spiritual questions. Yet concern for integration between the personal and the collective in spirituality has concerned some secular philosophers as well. Indeed, writing from a secular humanist perspective, Foucault, in *The Hermeneutics of the Subject,*[9] weaves the ramifications of differentiating between philosophy as "know thyself" and spirituality as "care of self" throughout his historical study of knowledge. He develops the advice of Plato that if one wants to be involved in political life one must take care of one's self. Foucault traces how the various disciplines for developing spiritually, disciplines like reflection, meditation on mortality, caring for the self and so on were followed even by non-theists throughout history. Now, while Foucault does not support a theistic orientation to spirituality, his argument does provide a humanistic framework for spirituality as the integration of the personal and the political, which is the path of spiritual education so needed within Canadian schools.

The humanist approach to contemplation-in-action is not the same, necessarily, as that held by religious adherents. Obviously, the theistic horizon of meaning, which provides the ground and the goal for religious approaches to contemplation-in-action, is not shared by secular humanists. What is shared, however, is a common appreciation for the epistemology of contemplation and the need to pursue an integration of both the contemplative and active dimensions of life. If we keep in mind the goal of turning the soul to the world then joining together religious and secular energies to serve our Canadian soul and the world soul can help to release a dynamism for good that would have a significant impact.

An epistemology of contemplation allows for the integration of the rational way of knowing and the spiritual way of knowing. Contemplation, in fact, requires both ways in order to be complete. When contemplating, I must pay attention through my senses to the ground of being in life, to the reality that runs below the surface of life, to the "hidden wholeness"[10] that lies at the center of the world. Contemplation requires that I savour the experience of the real world as a door to the *more* in life and that I listen intuitively to the experience of oneness and unity. It also requires that this experience shed light upon my understanding and my intelligence. Thus, the attentiveness to the soul of the world informs my cognitive intelligence. The co-natural way of knowing and rational way of knowing interconnect and lead to contemplative knowledge. When contemplation is integrated along with the experiences that arise from the active life, we have a method of spiritual knowing that is found in both secular and religious locations.

This contemplative-in-action spirituality, found within world religions and secular humanism, has been given renewed expression in recent years within education circles most notably through the work of Parker Palmer. According to Palmer, action and contemplation are not contradictory states of being or opposites "but poles of a great paradox that can and must be held together."[11] According to him, the source of the human drive to action and contemplation is the same: the desire to be alive and to celebrate the gift of life itself.[12] In order to overcome any unhealthy distancing between the contemplative and active dimensions, Palmer suggests that we place hyphens between the words and speak of contemplation-and-action. These hyphens would better connote the truth of human life that neither dimension can truly exist without the other. But I would go even further and change the *and* to *in* so that contemplation-and-action becomes contemplation-in-action in keeping with following the insight of St. Ignatius. St. Ignatius argued that we must bring our contemplation to our action and our action to our contemplation. In linking these two dimensions in such an integral fashion, Ignatius knew that it was both false and unhealthy to suppose that each dimension was somehow independent and autonomous. In truth, there is mutuality between the contemplative and active dimensions, one that is reciprocally beneficial. This link allows for a more complete integration of the contemplative and action dimensions within the person seeking to grow within a community aligned with the good.

Palmer argues that there are three stages in the development of contemplation-and-action: separation, alternation, and integration. In the first stage, contemplation and action are seen as separate. In the second stage, a person alternates between contemplative practices and active engagement. In the third stage, a person achieves a certain degree of integration of these two dimensions so that one is active when contemplating and contemplating during action. At this stage, the previous paradox of apparent opposites between these two dimensions yields to a holism founded upon the desire for life, or what I would call living from the soul. The desire for life, the longing for soul, is grounded upon the hidden wholeness that lies beneath everyday life.[13] The reciprocity and complementarity between contemplation and action has the effect of assisting us in achieving a holistic approach to spiritual living. Contemplation helps us to live creatively and action helps us to live contemplatively.

In our day and in our context we need to understand contemplative-in-action spirituality as requiring our attentiveness towards the soul found in all creation, both natural and human, and in our engaging in political actions that promote and sustain the presence of soul in creation, both natural and human. Moreover, as Canadians we need to be attentive to the currents of the Canadian soul that flow all around us, in us, and through us. Contemplation-in-action involves the seeking of the life energy that flows from the soul, as well as pursuing actions that sustain the soul in all its dimensions. Thus, a Canadian contemplative-in-action seeks to promote the common ground that we share as Canadians. This approach to integrating the active and contemplative dimensions of life is something that both religious and secular educators can support as they seek to teach for a more humane and sustainable future. This traditional method is one that is appropriate for educating for civic spirituality and, because it is free of explicitly religious or secular connotations, can be easily adapted within Canadian educational practice. This method provides the pedagogy for engaged spirituality, a spirituality which brings the Canadian soul to the front of the classroom and which is needed today across Canadian schools in order to ensure the vitality Canada of as a nation during this time of tremendous historical change.

ENGAGED SPIRITUALITY

Engaged spirituality seeks to bring the social and political concerns of life into our spiritual journey. It encourages the political and the mystical simultaneously and sees both dimensions of life as fundamental arenas for personal attention and communal focus. As any spiritual teacher knows, the active life includes anything from breathing, to reflecting and writing, from simple actions (like washing dishes and manual labour) to more complex actions like social, political and environmental actions. The active life extends from personal breath to public politics and includes everything in between.

Thich Nhat Hanh, the Vietnamese Buddhist monk, has given voice to this understanding through his call for mindfulness in ordinary life, particularly everyday life as experienced in poverty or war situations.

> When I was in Vietnam, so many of our villages were being bombed. Along with my monastic brothers and sisters, I had to decide what to do. Should we continue to practice in our monasteries, or should we leave the meditation halls in order to help the people who were suffering under the bombs? After careful reflection, we decided to do both—to go out and help people and to do so in mindfulness. We called it engaged Buddhism. Mindfulness must be engaged. Once there is seeing, there must be acting. Otherwise, what is the use of seeing? [14]

What the socially-engaged contemplative knows is that the active life must include the active dimension of social service and political action. Hence, social critique, community development, social justice, political protest, and alternative living are constitutive ingredients for a fully integrated spiritual life in our time. Both service, as an expression of compassion, and political action, as a vehicle for addressing systems, are brought into the field of concern of the engaged contemplative. Essentially, engaged spirituality brings social and political activity for the betterment of the world into the horizon of concern for a person or a community seeking to live a spiritual life. Engaged spirituality is a social and political spirituality. It is a mystical and political spirituality that has a distinctively radical orientation if we understand radical as returning to the roots of one's communal soul. It is radical in that it includes a preferential attentiveness to those areas of life where the disenfranchised, the marginalized, and the poor are excluded from the benefits of the *anima mundi*. Engaged spirituality brings the heart of service to the communal realm where politics, economics, and social structures need refining, transforming, and correcting so that room is created for the positive currents of the soul to flow and give life. Engaged spirituality is in keeping with other movements in our world that integrate the personal and the political within spirituality. Ghandi's *satyagraha*[15] or truth force is a prime example of engaged, political spirituality.

Engaged spirituality is a path that seeks to respond to our emerging consciousness today, given that our social and political actions for justice must be united under a new ecological awareness of the earth as our home. Indeed, thanks to thinkers like Thomas Berry[16] and Canada's own David Suzuki,[17] we are better able to situate the works for social and political action within a new cosmological awareness of the earth as our shared home. Ecologists have drawn our attention to the presence of the sacred and the holy within our natural environment. They have challenged the preoccupation of many world religions with other worldly divine images that prevent the appreciation and care of the natural world. The soul of the world is present in, with, and through the world and we need to attend to its transparent presence. Thus, any sentient being who is without a home in the universe (the homeless in Canadian cities, the refugees arriving at our shores, the salmon and the cod, and other species that are vanishing in our time) deserves our compassionate attention. Such compassion must be matched with discerned action to shift our political will along the Canadian axis of justice in such a way that our communal policies and resources align with sustaining life for all. Including environmental, social and political concerns will shape our Canadian spiritual curriculum.

A spiritual curriculum involves making the connection between social/political justice and care of the environment, and the development of personal interiority and attitudes, so that both dimensions are bound together within a soulful understanding of life. It involves educating for actions that express our compassion for the natural world in which we live and breathe and have our being, and to pursue justice within the social systems we have constructed to enable us to abide together across our vast Canadian landscape. It includes an awareness that the bodily/physical world is connected to our spiritual consciousness and that any break in this connection leads to estrangement and decline. Ultimately, engaged spirituality is a way of being spiritually political. It is a civic or public spirituality. Following this spiritual path can help to promote, protect and magnify our Canadian soul and help students to deepen their identity as citizens and members of a national project worth investing in.

THE PATH OF ENGAGED SPIRITUALITY

The path of engaged spirituality[18] is rooted in the awareness that our journey through life is most comprehensive when it embraces tradition and innovation, charity and justice, care of self and care of others within just institutions.[19] Some people find support for this journey in the traditions of world religions. Others find support in secular philosophies of the spirit. When both religious and secular education systems bring the best from their traditions and seek to align these with the best currents of the Canadian soul (nature, inclusion, justice, compassion, and compromise) we have the foundations for Canadian spiritual education. Moreover, when both religious and secular streams of education collaborate on actions that promote the soul of Canada, we witness the impact that such a spirituality can have.

Bringing the currents of the Canadian soul to the forefront of our educational practice requires an educational philosophy of spirituality that enables this project. The philosophy of engaged spirituality provides the necessary theoretical framework for such an undertaking. Generally there are seven insights that can be gathered from the path of engaged spirituality. These insights provide signposts or guidelines for the promotion of this Canadian civil spirituality.

i) First Insight: Interconnectivity

The first insight is that all of creation is connected and that the many different parts of creation mutually affect each other. There is a fluidity of energy, a symbiosis of cause and effect that permeates all of reality. Thus, touching one part of the real has an effect upon other parts of reality. Conversely, we can feel in the particularity of one local reality the impact of larger, global and universal realities when these blow through. The universal and the local, the distant and the close, the natural world and the worlds of human creation, are all connected and influence each other.

As we have watched the mounting evidence of climate change rooted in human activity we know that this interconnectivity and mutuality is true of the natural world. We have seen the evidence of climate change across our vast land. The evidence is now considered irrefutable amongst Canadians. We know now that our polluting practices are impacting upon our climate and that climate changes are in turn impacting upon our quality of life. With the aid of satellite imagery, computerized tracking and forecasting, and scientific research we can see the impact, which human population trends, urban sprawl, deforestation, fossil fuel dependency, and so forth have upon our fragile ecosystem. Indeed, in many ways this first signpost of engaged spirituality is already operative within our present day consciousness. It is omnipresent in our news and we feel it in the changing climate in which we seek to live and grow.

Another area where we see the principle of interconnectivity and mutuality operative is in the Canadian multicultural society of today. Here we see how different cultures and races work together and shape each other. Often it is the realm of economics that brings different cultures today and this is the gift of economics. Sometimes it is only the peripheral elements of cultures that interact. Sometimes it is the heart of the cultures that come together. Multicultural festivals are moments where we can experience the positive energy that accumulates when differences are celebrated. The exchange that takes place between cultures and races can be mutually beneficial. There is often a dynamism that flows when differences are allowed to live and be celebrated. Celebrating such diversity feeds the sense of belonging to the larger community for through celebrations we more easily experience our unity in diversity.

The insights of interconnectivity and mutuality are not only revealed, how-ever, when we attend to the realities of the external life of creation and world event. They are also core components of the engaged spiritual life. That is, the active life of social and political engagement and the reflective personal life required for personal wellbeing are connected and, while calling for differ-ent energies, mutually impact upon each other. One could say that the inner universe of reflective interiority and the outer universe of social and political action are first cousins whose lineage can be traced back to creation itself. In fact, the worlds of psychology, physics, mathematics, and literature all point to how integral the inner and outer dimensions of life actually are. This insight of connection and mutuality yields an appreciation for relationships and holism. Thus, the reflective and active dimensions of life are related and when pursued together promote holism, peace, and harmony. Indeed, these two dimensions function best when they embrace each other.

ii) Second Insight: Progressive Transformation

The second insight arising from engaged spirituality is that there is con-tinual development and transformation in personal consciousness, the natural world, and in human civilization. Nature and society are in continual trans-formation and growth. Despite the real evidence around us of social systems in decline and the extinction of numerous species there remains, when seen from the long arc of history, plenty of evidence to support the awareness that nature and society are in progressive and continual transformation. From the starbursts that birthed the galaxies billions of years ago to the global and his-torical consciousness that permeates the earth today, we can see movement, transformation, and expansion of energy. This insight leads to a conviction that even if the human species dies out somehow, the energy born from the human species will continue to creatively circulate in perhaps unimaginable ways. The future embedded in the insight of progressive development coun-teracts fear with a hope grounded in a reading of history that is progressive rather than regressive.

Canada, although a young nation relatively speaking, is a good example of development and transformation. We have changed a great deal as a na-tion since the days when First Nations alone populated these lands. From the pre-conquest days to today the changes are immense. From the building of the Canadian national railway, to the creation of ten provinces and three territories, to the mobile workforce of today, we have witnessed tremendous changes. Our change from a bicultural to a multicultural nation is also evi-dence of growth and development. Granted, there is ample evidence as well of how we have negatively impacted upon this vast land. In particular the

European maltreatment of our aboriginal peoples remains a constant reminder of our collective shadow. Still, over the long arc of Canadian history, we can see progress has been made on many fronts and such progress can form the foundation for a hopeful Canadian future.

The insight of continuous, progressive development and transformation grounds engaged spirituality as a pedagogy of hope. It is a hope born from the observance of history and the cosmos. Indeed, one of the fruits of engaged spirituality is the awareness that there is a river of grace running through the past, the present, and the future. Engaged spirituality, then, operates from a progressive view of history and is oriented towards a hopeful future. It builds up, rather than tears down and in doing so inspires rather than deflates, which is the weakness of much deconstructive pedagogy.

iii) Third Insight: Small Actions Create Change

The third insight is that true lasting social and political change for the common good takes place through the accumulation of many apparently small actions. Those who are spiritually engaged see the importance of addressing systemic and political structures so as to bring about changes that will result in justice and sustainability within Canada. They also see how important it is to make small lifestyle changes and to slowly build transformative local communities where the concerns of ecology, justice, compassion, openness, and an appreciation for compromise and ambiguity are given space to grow. Finally, they also see attending to changes in one's own heart and attitude as important to the work of bringing the best of the Canadian soul into the light of day. This pedagogy of small actions contributes to the building and healing of our nation, the global community, and the earth as well.

We see evidence of this pedagogy of small, deliberate steps in the women's movement, which has spanned the last century. Over time and through many small steps there has emerged a substantive and qualitative change for the lives of women in our country. The steady improvement in working conditions over the years is due to the accumulated actions of Canada's organized labour movement. The recent historical apology offered to our First Nations by our government is result of many small steps for meaningful recognition taken over the years. Finally, the adaptation of Canada's progressive Charter of Rights and Freedoms is a testimony to the work of intellectuals, politicians, and citizens to work together to craft legislation that would contribute immensely to Canadian society. There is ample evidence within Canada's history of how slow and steady progress on issues ultimately resulted in changes that have improved the lives of all Canadians.

To be spiritually engaged, then, means to have a heart that beats with the hope and the realization that each and every small action directed towards the *anima mundi* has an impact upon the nation and the world. Furthermore, each attitude held within a person and offered through the heart has an impact upon our national soul. Indeed, we know how anger or gratitude have very different effects upon community and give rise to different modes of action for change. The insight of change through small actions, when combined with the insight of structural changes resulting from consistently right actions, yields an appreciation for the wisdom of long-term engagement.

iv) Fourth Insight: Unity and Diversity Coexist

The fourth insight that arises from spiritual engagement is that unity and diversity, community and individuality, wholeness and fragmentation, exist simultaneously. This is essentially the insight that through all of creation there flows the soul of the world, which is an energy that gives life. Such an insight arises frequently during times of quiet recollection and rest but it can also happen in the whirlwind of action for the person who is attentive and living in congruence with his or her deepest truth. One holds together these seemingly incompatible awarenesses as one dances the way of spiritual engagement. Such awareness calls for maturity in spiritual life. It calls for an ability to hold the tensions between apparent contradictions in life, to look for a "hidden wholeness"[20] that lies below and between divisions. It calls for an ability to attend to the soul that flows through life and to accept the responsibility that we are all soul keepers.

This principle, in a practical sense, grounds our Canadian experience of growing multiculturalism. Through the sometimes hidden wholeness of our common bond as Canadians, we are able to accept the diversity of cultures within our nation. From a stance of being held together by a common bond, our national soul, we are able to see and embrace the reality that a diversity of cultures makes Canada a vivacious and beautiful place to be. The co-existence of a common soul and a diversity of cultures provides evidence of the creative tension between unity and difference. The creative tension does not lead to the eradication of either unity or diversity but simply adds energy to our Canadian soul.

v) Fifth Insight: Realism

The fifth insight is that engaged spirituality is realistic rather than naïve. If the twentieth century taught us anything, it was to mistrust any ideologies or agendas for achieving utopia. The same applies to any approach to spirituality as a definitive and final answer to life's challenges and our social problems.

Quite the contrary, a spiritual approach to life calls for a humble realism and acceptance of limits. Engaged spirituality helps to prepare people to avoid naïve optimism by assisting people in learning how to accept and integrate failure, suffering, evil and corruption. It requires that we teach ways to realistically move towards the future such that we work towards the new out of the shell of the old. This pedagogy is not so much revolutionary as transformational. That is, it does not seek to overturn the established order necessarily for it recognizes, albeit in a critical way, the gifts of history and tradition. Yet, it is a transformational pedagogy in that it seeks to bring the new out of whatever is empty in the shell of the old. This is because real, meaningful and constructive change necessarily entails being incarnated within human systems if that change is going to endure. We live our spiritual lives in the midst of human systems, which, for all their gifts and limitations, provide the context for the expression of our soul.

Seasoned teachers know the wisdom of approaching change in realistic ways. Those who have taught under different governments know that educational policies and directives come and go with the will of the government. As politically driven educational changes come and go, the experience in the field helps to separate the wheat from the chaff. There is a little good and a little bad in most educational policies. Wise teachers ensure that it is the good that is retained. Wisdom comes from knowing that the best education is one that includes three movements: transmission, transaction, and transformation of knowledge.[21] During the transmission movement, core knowledge is transmitted from the teacher to the student. This retention of the good is the traditional approach to learning. The second movement, the transaction movement, allows for a dialogical interchange to take place between the teacher and the student so that both learn something. This exchange is a more liberal approach to learning. The third movement, often named as the radical approach, seeks to stress how the knowledge learned can be used to help increase the personal good and the common good. These three movements are apropos for the teaching of spirituality for there can be a conservative movement (transmission), a liberal movement (transaction) and a radical movement (transformational) in spirituality. Thus, education for spirituality will include the insights of conservatives, liberals, and radicals, judging each on the ability to facilitate engagement with the currents of the Canadian soul in ways that build up rather than tear down.

vi) Sixth Insight: A Communal Path

The sixth insight is that the pursuit of this spiritual path is not an individual task but rather one shared with others. We live in a culture that champions the autonomous individual, and there is much good in this turn towards the individual in our times. It certainly has been a corrective to the stifling nature of some communal experiences whether these are cultural, religious, or both. The Québécois experience of the Catholic Church prior to the Quiet Revolution is an example of how stifling some communal forces can be. More recently, the debate over the acceptance of Sharia law in Ontario is another example of how Canadians reject any communal force that suppresses the rights of the person. Indeed, the Canadian Charter of Rights and Freedoms is a testament to the priority given to the individual within our social imagination. Maintaining a balance between the rights of the individual and the rights of society continues to challenge our courts. The very fact that our courts grapple with this problem is an indication that we recognize that the human person does not stand alone but is a person in community and that there is a shared sense of obligation to society.

Engaged spirituality stands upon a conviction that the human being is a person rather than an individual. In Western literary lore, the quintessential individual is Robinson Crusoe, the Lone Ranger, or one who lives without the need of others. From a spiritual perspective, however, a person becomes a human being through relationships and community. Indeed, the success of the engaged spiritual path hinges on the cumulative work of the person in community. It presumes the reality of solidarity with others, within systems, and with the natural world. This community base for personal spirituality is more participatory, democratic, and emancipatory than hierarchal and repressive communal structures of the past. So, the way of engaged spirituality is a method that is rooted in community and nature and in the shared knowledge and wisdom that arises out of shared work. In order to educate for this path we need to find ways to give expression to this communal dimension, ways that will have a ceremonial or ritual element to them.

Let me provide an example from my own professional life. Years ago I attended a three-day conference on global education. The conference was held in an outdoor centre, near the St. Lawrence River, during early November. Throughout our days I would walk outside whenever I could. It was sunny and warm for November and I felt drawn to be out as much as I could. As I walked I noticed tall, old oak trees yielding their acorns for the new life that was destined to follow the cold winter to come. I started to collect the acorns, planning to use them when I returned to school in small class ceremonies to accompany the famous National Film Board film, *The Man Who Planted Trees*. The end of the conference included a closing ceremony, which was held outside. This ceremony included the blessing and chants of a visiting First Nations elder and our standing together in a large circle around smoldering sweet grass. As part of the closing ceremony committee, I passed out to each participant an acorn and invited him or her to plant the seeds of what they had learned in the hearts of their students. In this small ritual, we celebrated the communal aspect of engaged spirituality in a way that respected the different horizons of meaning of the different participants. We allowed nature to provide us with symbols, acorns, to nourish us on our journey.

vii) Seventh Insight: Acceptance of Finitude

The seventh and final insight found within engaged spirituality is that there is a humble acceptance of the finitude of human capacity for transformation and change. We, as human beings, are limited, finite, and fallible creatures. Hence, our ability to act and our ability to reflect are not infinite. We are unable to come to absolute truths, although we may pursue them. Anyone who has sought to pursue spiritual engagement could share experiences of frustration, discouragement, and even depression that accompany times when one meets the defeat of a political action, the apparent continuation of injustice in the world, or the magnitude of the task to bring about systemic change. Such situations of limit are a constitutive part of the human journey and need to be addressed within any spirituality, including engaged spirituality, which seeks to integrate the social and political with the personal. In particular, we need to be careful when introducing children to this method and to use age-appropriate curriculum. We do not want to inadvertently do harm or fail to prepare them for the fact that disappointments and setbacks are normal in the spiritual life.

Given the realities of schooling today across Canada, from kindergarten to university, and the minimal time and resources currently being allocated to spiritual education, the truth is that teachers who seek to integrate spirituality within their practice will have plenty of experiences with limit situations. These may be financial, resource, time, or personnel limits. But, key to the embrace of these limits will be our attitude. If we think that the spiritual life is not channeled through the real and the practical exigencies of everyday life then we are misinformed. The truth is that engaged spirituality recognizes that the soul finds expression in the concrete realities of life and that the limits of human life provide the shape and the form for the soul. Teachers of engaged spirituality will seek opportunities to teach for an integration of the Canadian soul with the personal self in whatever ways they can find in their particular context and within their specific limits. This approach will demand creativity and inspiration, but thankfully most teachers are very imaginative and therefore capable of integrating spirituality into their subject matter.

CONCLUSION

Canadian educators are, in many ways, in a blessed context. Living in a country where diverse religions coexist within a secular framework, we are able to take the best from these religious traditions and use them in our professional activities. Moreover, secular educators are able to contribute their insights to how to best educate for an intelligent and responsive spirituality while learning from the best of religious traditions. The contemplative-in-action path borrowed from religious traditions and resonating with some secular humanist philosophies, can provide an appropriate method for a healthy civil spirituality for Canadians. Reconstructed as engaged spirituality, contemplation-in-action can be a method for use within Canadian schools regardless of their religious or secular orientation. The seven insights for this method can be easily integrated across various disciplines and used to inform everyday professional practice, as well as the administration of Canada schools today. This method can be a way of engaging, promoting, and magnifying the Canadian soul, which pulses across our landscape. In addition to the seven insights for engaged spirituality there are a variety of strategies and practices that accompanying this method, which can be incorporated within Canadian education. Let us now turn our attention to these strategies and practices.

NOTES

1. Diarmuid O'Murchu, *Reclaiming Spirituality: A New Framework for Today's World* (New York, NY: The Crossroad Publishing Company, 1998), pp. 12–13.

2. See: *The Heart of Learning: Spirituality in Education*, ed. Steven Glazer (New York: Jeremy P. Tarcher/Putman Publisher, 1999) and *Holistic Learning and Spirituality in Education: Breaking New Ground*, ed. John P. Miller (Albany, NY: State University of New York Press, 2005). Throughout both texts, various well known public intellectuals wade into the area of spirituality in secular public education. Such voices include: Parker J. Palmer, Dzogchen Ponlop Rinpoche, The Dalai Lama, bell hooks, David Orr, Diana Chapman Walsh, Huston Smith, Vincent Harding, Thomas Moore, Riane Eisler, John P. Miller, and others.

3. Parker Palmer, *To Know As We Are Known: A Spirituality of Education* (San Francisco: Harper and Row, 1983).

4. Thomas Groome, *Educating For Life: A Spiritual Vision for Every Teacher and Parent* (Allen, Texas: Thomas More, 1998).

5. Edmund O'Sullivan, *Transformative Learning: Educational Vision for the 21st Century* (Toronto: University of Toronto Press, 1999), pp.259–281.

6. David Suzuki and Amanda McConnell, *The Sacred Balance: Rediscovering Our Place in Nature* (Vancouver: Greystone Books, 1997).

7. Yusuf Ibish and Peter Wilson, eds, *Traditional Modes of Contemplation and Action: A Colloquim at Rothko Chapel, Houston Texas* (Great Britain: Billings and Son, 1977).

8. Donald W. Mitchell and James A. Wiseman, OSB, eds, *The Gethsemani Encounter: A Dialogue on the Spiritual Life by Buddhist and Christian Monastics* (New York: Continuum Publishing Company, 1999).

9. Michel Foucault, *The Hermeneutics of the Subject: Lectures at the College de France 1981–1982* (New York: Picador, 2001).

10. Parker Palmer, *The Active Life: Wisdom for Work, Creativity, and Caring* (San Francisco: HarperCollins, 1990), p. 29.

11. Ibid., p. 7.

12. Ibid., p. 15.

13. Ibid., p. 29.

14. Thich Nhat Hanh, *Peace Is Every Step: The Path of Mindfulness in Everyday Life*, edited by Arnold Kotler (New York: Bantam Books, 1991). p. 91.

15. "Truth (satya) implies love, and firmness (agraha) engenders and therefore serves as a synonym for force. I thus began to call the Indian movement 'satyagraha': that is to say, the force which is born of truth and love or nonviolence" in *The Words of Gandhi: Selected by Richard Attenborough* (New York, NY: Newmarket Press, 1982), p. 46.

16. Thomas Berry, *The Dream of the Earth* (San Francisco: Sierra Club Books, 1990).

17. David Suzuki and Amanda McConnell, *The Sacred Balance: Rediscovering Our Place in Nature* (Vancouver: Greystone Books, 1997).

18. For a more philosophical treatment of this path, see my book *Contemplation In Liberation: A Method for Spiritual Education in the Schools* (Lewiston, NY: Edwin Mellen Press. 2001), pp. 102–111.

19. While he does not deal directly with engaged contemplation Paul Ricoeur in *Oneself as Another* (Chicago: The University of Chicago, 1992) argues for a comprehensive approach to ethics as living well with and for others in just institutions.

20. Palmer, *The Active Life*, p. 29.

21. John P. Miller, *The Holistic Teacher* (Toronto: OISE Press, 1993), pp. 11–14.

Chapter Five

Teaching the Path

A soulful curriculum recognizes and gives priority to the inner life. It seeks a balance and connection between our inner and outer lives.[1]

One of the most creative examples of educating for spirituality in contemporary schools I ever experienced was the celebration of a day focused on healing and reconciliation. This healing day was an experimental attempt to break open the value of healing and reconciliation for students in ways that would speak to them. It was a day when we could focus on the various areas of life, which require healing and reconciliation with students. This generation of students is acutely aware of the reality of suffering, brokenness, and hurt that exists in our world. As chaplain, I worked closely with the Student Services department of our school and with a core group of student leaders. There was considerable preparation required for the success of this day, but it was worthwhile.

Central to the success of the day was the fact that we used a cross-curricular approach. We identified a variety of themes that connected to the concept of healing and reconciliation. These included the personal, familial, physical, communal, economic, political, religious, cultural, global, environmental, and spiritual areas of life. About a month prior to the day, we approached the leaders of each department and invited them to choose a theme and to integrate the topics of healing and reconciliation within their subject matter in whatever way they saw fit. The vision was that on healing day students would be exposed to the themes of healing and reconciliation in each and every class they attended and would learn various ways of addressing these topics depending upon the particular subject matter and their grade level. This cross-curricular approach to healing and reconciliation allowed for a truly comprehensive and holistic learning experience. The success of the curriculum component of the day depended solely upon the creativity and ingenuity of the department heads and individual teachers; it was truly amazing how individual teachers rose to the challenge to teach about healing and reconciliation when the window of opportunity presented itself.

Concurrent with the curriculum delivery of these concepts, we made a few changes to the daily routine. We played songs over the PA system, which the students felt spoke to the focus of the day and included short readings of leaders who had worked to create a better world. We also had a voluntary ritual in the atrium at the center of the school where students could drop by throughout the day and give expression to their many and varied ways of participating in healing and reconciliation. Over several years, we accumulated mementoes of the day and displayed them permanently in the school as a reminder of our healing days in the school.

These days required some advanced preparation for a core group of teachers and students and a little adaptation to the specific curriculum over which each teacher presided. The differentiated teaching allowed for differentiated learning, which led to there being a creative excitement in the school, an excitement that pointed to the presence of soul. Indeed, student participation was always very high and the lively ways in which some teachers brought their subject matter to deal directly with the values of healing and reconciliation was inspiring. Healing day stands out in my mind as a prime example of how spirituality can be integrated into the life of a busy school. Using cross-curricular approaches to spiritual themes, involving teachers and students in planning and implementation, and incorporating appropriate reflections, music, and ritual all with an eye to the creative and playful establishes a field in which spiritual education can be undertaken.

Healing day provides one example of how to educate for spirituality within the context of contemporary schools. There are many teachers across Canada trying new ways to break open the spiritual life for today's students. In this chapter, we will explore further some of the theoretical and practical considerations for spiritual education in Canadian schools to support such initiatives.

Good teachers keep one eye on theory and their subject matter and another eye on students and the classroom. Good teachers bring both loci of their vision together into a focused attentiveness that enables the classroom to become a place of soulful learning. Good teachers are those who are able to convey to students their love for theory and content as well as their enjoyment of being in the classroom with students. Their aliveness to the subject matter and to their students is infectious and facilitates the learning experience. The teacher who is able to provide a safe, friendly learning environment where students are invited into learning is a teacher well worth their weight in gold. The ability to teach in this way is something that accrues over time and with experience. By being open to learning while they teach, teachers can become guides for turning the soul to the world.

This ability to provide the contexts for learning is especially important to the teaching of the path of engaged spirituality. I have already discussed how there is a need for spiritual education across Canada and that spiritual knowing needs to be brought into the mainstream way of knowing (that of intellect and power), so as to provide a holistic and wisdom centered learning. I have suggested that we need to make room for an education in the Canadian soul, a soul that is rooted in Canadian history and which, with its many different yet mutually beneficial currents, can provide energy for our future as a nation. Furthermore, I have offered that the traditional method of contemplation-in-action can serve as an appropriate method for spiritual education within Canada's growing secular and religiously pluralistic country. The insights for engaged spirituality discussed in the previous chapter provide us with some theoretical directions for such an education.

We now turn to some pedagogical considerations that need to be kept in mind as we teach for engaged spirituality, across the span of Canadian schooling from kindergarten to post-secondary and from coast to coast to coast. Some teachers might prefer an actual curriculum or even a textbook to guide them. These resources will not be offered for the following reasons. First, the path of engaged spirituality is a way of educating and it is to be followed across disciplines and throughout life. Hence, it would be difficult to provide in this short book a guide for how to educate for this path in each subject and each grade level. One would require teams of curriculum writers to achieve this goal. My experience with the healing day approach convinced me that teachers have within their own repertoire the skills, knowledge, and expertise to make the spiritual come to life in their own classrooms. In fact, the possession of such skills, knowledge, and expertise is the art of teaching. Spiritual education ultimately depends upon the creative and artistic life of the teacher.

Second, most teachers and students are already swamped with too many expectations. It would be futile to add to these expectations without taking away something. Spiritual education should not be an onerous imposition to teaching practice but rather an orientation that permeates the entire educational project. What teachers can do is follow the path of engaged spirituality in their personal and professional lives and thereby become role models and coaches of this path. Indeed, central to the success of spiritual education is the life and witness of the teacher. If a teacher's soul is turned to the world, it is likely that their professional practice will manifest this orientation. Indeed, their presence in the classroom will witness to this turn to the world.

Third, spirituality ultimately resists being pinned down for there will always be the ineffable and the mysterious accompanying those on the spiritual path. Such is the reality of seeking the *more* in everyday life. It would be foolish then to provide iron cast learning objectives and firm rules for this path of spiritual education. The approach here is to point in a direction, to open the heart of the learner to the sounds and sights of the spiritual life as mediated through the path of engagement in the currents of Canadian soul and to enable and permit students to pursue this path of learning.

While it is not the intention here to provide curriculum for this path there are nonetheless several considerations for the teaching the way of engaged spirituality that deserve our attention. I will first discuss the larger framework concerning spiritual formation as a life long journey. Then I will discuss the method for spiritual education that can be integrated into each level of education. I will leave it up to teachers to imagine how they could integrate this method within their areas of responsibility.

THE PATH AS A LIFE JOURNEY

The way of engaged spirituality is a path that can be followed throughout one's life, from school age to old age.[2] Developmental theorists, consciousness-raising theorists, and philosophers each have something to say about life as a journey. Let us consider these insights since they provide the background for educating students in the spiritual life.

DEVELOPMENTAL CONSIDERATIONS

As good educators know the key to successful pedagogy is knowing not only what to teach but also when to teach it. This allows a teacher to break down knowledge into age appropriate steps so that the learner may progress in the appropriation of knowledge. Developmental theorists have much to offer as we consider educating for spirituality.

a) Psychology

In Canada, as in other Western societies, our educational practice has been heavily and properly influenced by developmental psychology. Leading psychological thinkers and researchers like Erikson, Piaget, and Kohlberg have each offered their different perspectives on the developmental approach to learning. Each has proposed stages or phases of maturation, which a person normally passes through as they journey from birth to death. Reflecting our cultural bias and sympathy for science, these approaches have helped to humanize our educational practice by demonstrating just how complex and multifaceted the process of learning actually is. These developmental approaches have also helped teachers to appreciate the developmental tasks of students at different ages thereby helping to enhance the relationship between teachers and students. Indeed, the incorporation of age appropriate teaching strategies and learning goals has been a positive contribution to modern education. They have helped to humanize our schools.

However, there are limits to these developmental approaches. First, some developmental theorists can tend to be too prescriptive and categorical thereby limiting the uniqueness of individual experiences. This tendency can lead to the danger of dismissing the individual student in our classroom or overlooking the uniqueness of their personality. Secondly, some stage developmental theorists tend to reveal an adult bias and to value the superiority of adults over children.[3] This bias can lead to a premature foreclosure on the insights and wisdom that can arise during the time of youth. Thirdly, some phased developmental approaches tend to be linear rather than cyclical. That is, they tend to fail to appreciate that much of learning, while sequential and progressive, requires a periodic revisiting and relearning of prior knowledge so as to grow in depth and wisdom. Wise teachers know better.

Despite these limitations, developmental theories do offer general outlines for understanding the learning process. They give teachers a broad understanding of the learning edges for their students and suggest avenues for consideration when delivering curriculum. The insights of developmental theorists are particularly important for creating the framework for spiritual education because the initial awe and wonder of childhood needs to be nurtured as a person travels the journey through life.

b) Religious Spirituality

When we turn to the various religious traditions in our world, we can see an appreciation as well for developmental approaches to the spiritual life. In fact, the psychological insights of modern times were in some ways prefigured by the spiritual insights of former times carried forth through world religions. We know that various world religions acknowledge that followers progress in their spiritual life and so offer various disciplines and guides for their respective paths. For our purposes here I shall limit my discussion to the insights from the Judeo-Christian tradition simply because it is the one that I am most familiar with. Readers who find meaning in another religious or spiritual tradition are encouraged to examine their own framework for guidance for spiritual growth to see how these can be integrated into teaching practice, and share their findings.

Spirituality within religion can generally be divided into two paths: the katphatic path, which is essentially the way of affirming images, concepts, and intellectual knowledge of God, and the apophatic path, which is essentially the way of journeying without the aid of images or concepts as one grows in experiential knowledge of God. The katphatic path relies heavily upon the doctrinal and ritual formulation of religious traditions, which is often safeguarded by sanctioned teachers or leaders. The apophatic path however relies heavily on direct spiritual experience. It is the mystical path, which is found within all world religions. Within the apophatic theology of Judeo-Christian spirituality, the developmental approach has traditionally been to see the spiritual life as consisting of three phases: the purgative, the illuminative, and the unitive. The classical voices of this path are St. John of the Cross, who wrote about the experience of the dark night, and St. Teresa of Avila, who wrote about the interior castle in which a person following the spiritual life roams. In addition to these classics we have the contemporary voice of Thomas Merton, the Trappist monk and writer who integrated the apophatic path within his thought and writing. The understanding of the spiritual life as a journey through different stages has been extremely helpful in the areas of spiritual direction over the centuries.

However, these approaches are sometimes distorted and misinterpreted by religious adherents. The most fundamental distortion within Christianity happens when some people focus too heavily on the notion of original sin as foundational to life. This starting point often leads people to overlook the innate goodness and beauty of our real world. Often it leads to a rejection of the world as sinful. When we fixate on sin as the prime foundation of life, rather than the goodness and beauty of creation, we end up with a spirituality that tends to be more negative than positive, one that focuses more on human failings than on human accomplishments. An unhealthy fixation on original sin often leads to a disdain for worldly affairs and to a preoccupation with an afterlife, rather than the present life. This fixation is one of the major critiques of religious spiritualities that come from secular humanists. The secular critique of original sin forces religious advocates to clarify their worldviews. It asks them to take into account the historical and scientific evidence of creation and to incorporate a healthier appreciation of the role of the creative and natural world in terms of spirituality. Diarmuid O'Murchu, a counselor and social psychologist in London, in *Reclaiming Spirituality*, has written about this need to bring the insights of science into our understanding of spirituality.[4] O'Murchu argues that including the scientific approach within our spiritual way of knowing can only help to expand, deepen, and renew our spiritual life.

One of the religious pioneers in a reframing of the Christian apophatic path is Matthew Fox. Fox argues that we need to see the spiritual journey through life as including four, rather than three, stages. The first stage is the *via positiva*, one where we begin with our location in the created world which is full of beauty, diversity and life. Cosmologist Brian Swimme and eco-theologian Thomas Berry have also added to this insight by calling attention to the narrative of cosmogenesis wherein the universe itself is seen to be in a continuous process of becoming.[5] During the *via positiva* phase we experience elation, awe, wonder, and delight. This experience is a constitutive component of a truly holistic approach to spirituality. The second phase, the *via negativa*, is the one where we experience silence, suffering, sorrow, and grief. This experience often happens as we grow and mature, for life includes suffering, misadventure, loss, and death. We cannot avoid the fact that suffering is a part of human life. Nobody has a monopoly on suffering. Neither is it distributed equally. Religions of the world, in particular Buddhism and Christianity, try to address suffering in meaningful ways. The third phase is that of *via creativa*. In this stage people invest themselves in creative work that gives expression to the self. They invest in family, relationships, power, and wealth. In many ways, we in Western culture exemplify this phase. The final phase is that of *via transformativa*. In this phase, the person turns their energy towards building systems that help to transform the world.[6]

Fox, in calling our attention to the primal goodness and beauty of creation, adds a positive foundation to the traditional understanding of spiritual development. This reformulation is helpful, for it allows us to build a life affirming spirituality that is creation-centered and one that affirms responsible human action as part of spiritual life. Moreover, Fox's amplification of the spiritual path as grounded upon an original beauty and blessing helps to form the foundations for a dialogue between religious and non-religious approaches to spiritual education. That is, while there might be disagreements regarding the causes of suffering in our world, there can be agreement on the inherent goodness of human life and creation and the need to promote common actions that preserve this goodness. Such an orientation can be helpful when our students bring their suffering into our classroom.

While Fox is right in the need to correct the traditional religious preoccupation with sin, I think we need to adopt the same cautious eye to his developmental approach as we do to those of developmental theorists. We must not naïvely laud the concept of original blessing in such a way that we are blind to the reality of destruction, suffering, and sin in the world.

In truth, we must be careful not to universalize spiritual development and demand that every person proceed in the same fashion. We also must avoid any hierarchy of phases so that we do not value any one of these phases over the other. This hierarchy can lead to an overvaluing of adults in the spiritual life. It can lead to elitism in spirituality. This elitism would be unfortunate: in my own experience, I have learned just as much about the spiritual life from children, teenagers, and young adults as I have from adults. When we share our journeys as pilgrims we have much to learn from each other. I do feel that the developmental approach is valid and a good description of the spiritual path if we see life developing progressively in a spiritual fashion. Thus, we slowly move forward but necessarily continue to return to old concerns with new insights until we are ready to move onto the next stage. The developmental approach to spirituality is especially appropriate for the way of engaged spirituality since on this path we try to integrate the social and political life with that of the personal and interior life. Such integration occurs only over time and often requires learning and relearning.

CONSCIOUSNESS-RAISING CONSIDERATIONS

We when turn to the area of education for social and political awareness, which is a constitutive part of engaged spirituality, we find the importance of recognizing the developmental approach as well. Paulo Freire has been a strong proponent of a process called conscientization, which has four phases. In the first phase, people are preoccupied with their physical needs and lack historical consciousness. The focus is on ensuring that the primary sources of life are present in order to provide a foundation for the human quest for the *more*. In the second phase, that of magical consciousness, we have the consciousness of closed societies. This consciousness is marked by a culture of silence where people take the socio-cultural facts of their lives as given. Here culture is very strong and people tend to be defensive, dependent, and fatalistic about their capacity to change things. The third stage, that of naïve consciousness, is often called "popular consciousness". Here people begin to question, but at a naïve or primitive level. People begin to see that they have the capacity to change their social and political contexts but this capacity is weakened by the felt sense of the need for popular leaders. Finally, Freire offers the fourth stage of critical consciousness. For Freire, this stage is the highest stage, one in which people learn and grow into political agency through dialogue and asking questions. During this stage, they become fully conscious and active. In this phase, people refuse to accept dehumanizing structures and instead move towards reflective social and political action.[7]

Freire's pedagogy of conscientization is one that is appropriate for Canadian educators, particularly as we deepen our understanding of our colonial past and its impact upon our national fabric. We are ever so mindful of the ills associated with our colonial roots. The legacy of our First Nations remains a constant teaching for us. If we are to avoid the worst of colonialism, we need to become more aware of our own imperialistic tendencies when dealing with others. We are now turning such awareness to our religious organizations in Canada and this is as it should be. We need to remain vigilant to ensure that a colonial or imperialist attitude does not take over our education for spirituality.

Again, while there is merit in Freire's approach, we need to be careful in being too prescriptive about learning. It is true that people do gradually grow in consciousness of the impact of social structures and their ability to change these structures. Yet, there are many factors that impede social and political change beyond that of the lack of consciousness. I have already alluded to the fact that the finitude of the human condition sometimes tempers our ability to act. We are finite creatures, full of potential, but also conditioned within our social, political, and cultural contexts. Another factor that can impede social and political change is that there are sometimes too few avenues to express and channel the energy for change. It has been my experience over the years that, by and large, people will put their energy and resources into the common good if they are presented with a clear and easy avenue. Thus, the challenge is to create vehicles and programs for channeling people's spiritual energy into the common good. This challenge is one of the reasons for consciously and intentionally bringing spirituality into our Canadian schools, to provide a path for the spiritual energy.

Despite the cautions of relying too heavily on developmental theories, whether psychological, religious, or political, I think that spiritual educators would do well to attend to the main insights of these theorists. Most certainly the insights for Freire regarding the development of critical consciousness of social and political factors is important for educators to learn and appropriate. Life is a journey, one through which we are invited to grow and mature. We need to respect where people are at in their journey. We are all pilgrims on this good earth. Moreover, we need to respect that this journey is lived out in community and in solidarity with other. Community and solidarity also influence the spiritual life. Incorporating psychological, philosophical, and political phases of learning into engaged spirituality is therefore an important task.

FUNDAMENTAL OPTION CONSIDERATIONS

In addition to understanding the developmental phases through which we all pass as we grow, develop and mature into responsible citizens we need to add an understanding of what, in philosophy, has been called the fundamental option. Briefly put, the philosophical notion of fundamental option, rooted in the thought of Thomas Aquinas, is the idea that each person must, at some point in their life, make a choice for others as a constitutive part of their self-identity. "The healthy fundamental option is openness to the Other and the others. It includes cooperative relationship in trust and self-transcending love."[8] This choice can be made at any point in a person's life once they have arrived at the point of reasoning, but it is a choice or an orientation that is usually made somewhere during the period of adolescence when, as Erikson says, identity is the key development task. Failure to make this choice often leads to a crippled adulthood and one will be forced to revisit the lack of choice throughout life until one makes a firm decision for others.

The option for others is considered fundamental because it goes to the heart of a person's spiritual orientation and forms the cornerstone to the development of their personality. That is, once someone has chosen to include others in their life they align subsequent actions with this choice, thereby co-creating their self within the social, political, religious, cultural, and economic contexts of their time. Through this fundamental option, a person's own conscience is formed.

This option for others can be a clear and definitive option consciously made in such a way that the person always remembers the moment of decision. It can be a diffuse and complicated option, weakly made, that one strengthens with subsequent choices and revisions throughout one's life. Whether strongly or weakly made, a fundamental option seeks the good of others as constitutive of one's own good in life. It shapes the spiritual orientation of a person.

The notion of a fundamental option complements the insights of developmental theorists. What the fundamental option offers is a pivotal reference point for spiritual development of the personality and for the education of the person. As the choice to align oneself with others grows to include the social, political, economic, and ecological dimensions of life, one's spiritual horizon widens as well. The fundamental option provides the core to spiritual formation and provides an axis from which a person can learn and discern which actions and attitudes are required for which situation. Quite rightly then, we can see that the formation of a fundamental option is important for the formation of our spiritual compass, that place within ourselves in which we balance the demands of the outer world and our inner life, the demands of justice and the requirements of our self, the development of our active life and our inner life. The fundamental option then is the choice to pursue the spiritual life and, in the case of engaged spirituality, the choice to pursue a spirituality that intentionally integrates social and political action with personal and interior growth.

Making the fundamental option for others, and allowing this option to be expressed through engaged spirituality, is always a personal choice. It is a choice that needs to be lived out, within community. It is nearly impossible for a person to live a life committed to engaged spirituality in a social milieu without the support of others. Teachers and parents know this concept well and encourage their students and children to choose their friends carefully. We all know that friends and peers can have a positive or a negative impact upon a person. This impact is all the more true in the spirituality of engagement because this is a spirituality that is communally based and presumes openness to and solidarity with others. Thus, a fundamental option must be lived individually and communally. The individual matures through including the concerns and needs of others into their life.

The fundamental option turns the person towards the world soul and connects their personal concerns with the concerns of others. It is an important learning threshold of personal spiritual formation that must be achieved in order for a person to be able to pursue the life of the soul, which is connected to the communal and world soul. In a sense, then, the promotion of the Canadian soul depends upon the facilitation of the fundamental option within citizens, an option that orients persons to others in self-transcendence.

THE PEDAGOGY OF ENGAGED SPIRITUALITY

For several years I organized a learning experience that enabled senior high school students to put their spirit into action. It was an Inner City Retreat in which the focus was to explore the issue of homelessness in Ottawa, Canada's capital. It started in response to the cuts to the social safety net during the mid-1990's as a way to educate students about the impact of poverty on individuals and the need to include vulnerable portions of our society into our political decisions.

The retreat ran for three days and included sleeping on the floor of a downtown church for two nights. Students were given a meager allowance from which to purchase their food, which they were able to cook together in a homeless women's center that served as our home base. During these days they visited various agencies serving the poor, worked in soup kitchens, listened to activists and rubbed shoulders with the homeless. Interspersed with these learning moments were times for quiet reflection, journaling, and group discussion. The intention of the retreat experience was simply to expose students to the reality of poverty in the middle of one of Canada's wealthiest cities and to connect them with the personal faces of this reality. Inevitably, the retreat was a transformative experience for many of the students, one in which their previous worldviews were challenged and broadened to include the needs of others who usually remain peripheral to our social imagination.

These Inner City Retreats were always a time of intense spiritual engagement. Throughout the days the active dimensions of service and political analysis intermingled with the contemplative dimensions of pondering and reflecting. Generally, participants' hearts were changed as their minds were filled with new experiences and stories. These retreats served as a concrete example of how to educate for engaged spirituality.

Teachers, equipped with the knowledge of developmental theories, whether psychological, spiritual or political, and with the crucial importance of nurturing the fundamental option for a soulful life nonetheless need practical pedagogical strategies if they are to be able to teach the way of engaged spirituality across various subjects and grade levels within a Canadian context. They require strategies that serve the pedagogy of engaged spirituality that can be integrated within their daily professional lives. The way of engaged spirituality provides such a method. There are four elements to this pedagogy of engaged spirituality: presence, discernment, engagement, and reflection.

Presence

The path of engaged spirituality is a path that incorporates the active dimension of social, political and ecological action; it is essentially a path that is rooted in being present to community. The soul of the community, and for our purposes here, the soul of Canada, provides the context for the living out of one's individual spiritual life. This notion of presence is based on a very traditional understanding of spirituality and one that goes against some strains of our secular modern mentality that praise the hegemony of the autonomous individual. Just as every parent knows the truth of the African proverb "It takes a village to raise a child," so too do we know that community forms the container for spirituality. Thus, we need to intentionally choose the attitude of presence. We need to be open to simply being with others, in relationship and in community.

Thus, this spiritual path is rooted in community as a prior condition. We recognize first that the pursuit of the national soul often involves social and political action. Such action is best accomplished with others, through community and for the benefit of the community, the nation. More particularly, this way often presumes solidarity with a marginalized group or issue,[9] such as with a group of people who are homeless or an issue with the environment. Solidarity is the stance of being with others and learning and listening to their needs, their hopes, and their limitations. The way of spiritual engagement, which seeks to bring the excluded and marginalized into the benefits of Canadian soul, is essentially a communal, other-directed spirituality, one that requires solidarity and fraternity.

The importance of community for engaged spirituality necessitates that we include two steps in this moment of presence. First, we need to put students in relationship with others. That is, we need to create the conditions for students to come to know the needs, hope, and limits of the community or group that they are to study or be engaged with. Such solidarity, fraternity, and connection can take place in different fashions. The success of the Inner City Retreats I ran depended upon these students coming into contact with homeless persons and learning through being present to others whose stories were different than theirs.

Teachers can do much to facilitate this moment of presence in different ways. First, they can identify a current of the national soul, which they feel they would like to address through engaged spirituality. Then, they can shape a moment of presence to the issues presented by the selected current. They may allow students to share their personal stories of the environment, injustice, or openness, for example. They might bring in guest speakers. They may bring students on field trips to places and situations where features of the Canadian soul are being lived or seeking expression. Students can take part in exchange programs in which they visit people in other parts of Canada or the world where the needs are great. The ways and means of this moment of presence are many and dependent upon the ingenuity and creativity of teachers. The key is to bring students into the presence of the *other* or *others* who are experiencing the current of the Canadian soul in either positive or negative ways.

Second, we need to teach and develop students' skills for communication. In this endeavour, active listening is an important skill to acquire. To be present and to listen with the heart to the needs of others is a spiritual practice. It is to listen to the world of the *other* so as to be able to be in empathic relationship. It is to hear their stories, whether it is the story of being homeless or being a new immigrant. It is to learn the facts concerning an endangered species or our fragile environment. We listen so as to hear more fully what the needs and concerns of the *other* actually are rather than what we think they should be. To do otherwise is to risk imposing solutions or ideas on situations that could potentially worsen the situation or enflame a volatile one. Not listening with the heart often leads to indoctrination and spiritual imperialism, neither of which serves the development of the soul, personal or national, in the long run.

Discernment

From the base experience of presence, students are then led into the moment of discernment. Discernment is a time-honored spiritual discipline in which we listen with the heart to the movement of the soul in our lives and in the lives of others. Discernment is a process wherein we use our imagination, our critical thinking skills, and our heart to move towards decisions that will advance the needs of the soul. Discernment can apply to our personal life. It can also apply to our communal and national soul.

In truth, we have already begun the process of discernment during the moment of presence because the first step of discernment is to gather data for deliberation. During the moment of presence we have, hopefully, learned more about what needs to happen to nurture the soul in others or in our nation at this point in time. Once we have gathered our data and read the signs of the time we seek to formulate the problem as best as we can. Here we develop the critical thinking skills of student. As good teachers know, it is important to ask the right question. A rightly posed question often helps to move a problem forward to a successful resolution or conclusion. Taking time to formulate questions and to brainstorm possible solutions to complex problems is essential to discernment.

The second step of discernment is to assess our own inner freedom or attachments. This step is much more than simply detecting personal or group bias. It is about moving through the attachments that get in the way of deep listening and openness to new learning. In this step we need to be mindful that there may be levels of freedom as we move from personal to group to national perspectives.

In order to facilitate our freedom, we need to ask certain questions. How are we individually and communally invested in the decision before us? What do we stand to gain? What do we stand to lose? Whose perspective is driving the issue at present? Whose needs and perspectives are left out? How attached are we to the issue and to either option in the decision? Furthermore, how is Canada invested in the decision before us? What do Canadians stand to gain or to lose? Which portion of Canadian society is driving the issue at present and which portion is being overlooked? How free are Canadians regarding the issue? These are not always easy questions to ask, but they can truly help to move students, both personally and as a group, to a greater freedom concerning the needs of the Canadian soul.

The third step in discernment is to use our imaginations and to imagine the implications of a particular choice. How does it look down the road? How does this option compare with the other options if they were lived out? What would Canada look like in several years, or generations, if a particular choice is implemented? Would the option being considered enhance the positives in the Canadian soul and bring peace and tranquility to the land or would it result in disorder and turbulence that causes harm? Our aboriginal brothers and sisters had the wisdom of asking what the implications of a choice would be seven generations down the line. Indeed, how might things have been different for our First Nations if Europeans had imagined the future in a different way than the violence of cultural assimilation that has become our legacy regarding Canada's aboriginals? These are ways in which the imagination can help in discernment. It utilizes our ability to forecast and predict and couples it with the imagination to create a vision that serves Canadians.

The fourth stage of discernment is the affective phase. Here, we need to listen to our feelings as we imagine the various ways of engaging the Canadian soul. Which way brings a sense of peace, excitement, hope, happiness and contentment? Which way leads to discord, discouragement, despair, and confusion? Sometimes the feelings are not always clear simply because the choices are hard and difficult. This lack of clarity will often be the case given the secular democratic reality of Canada and the burgeoning multicultural and multifaith composition of Canadians. Without this clarity, one needs to do the best that one can do, trusting in the inevitable progress of history. The reality of practicing a civil spirituality in a democracy is inherently complex and messy.

After having gathered the data, accessed our freedom and attachments, imagined the various options, and listened to our feelings, we then need to move towards making a decision. We try to bring the head and the heart together so that what we decide is both intelligent and wise: the ways of intellectual knowing and spiritual knowing come together. We breathe with both lungs, and we make a decision. Sometimes this decision will take time, for we need to learn to wait until the soul speaks. Then we need to implement the decision via our actions. These actions are often communal action. They may sometimes be individual actions that we can implement in our personal life.

Teaching and learning how to discern can have practical implications. It can help students to heighten their understanding of the impact of social systems and structures upon the Canadian soul, impacts which are not always known in the immediate context but which often require the passing of time to see the full implications. Using one's imagination to imagine the future of a particular line of social action and listening from the heart to the consequences for all partners, from ecosystems to local cultures, can help when deliberating over the wisdom of a particular systemic or collective action. Moreover, one can learn to recognize ways in which systems, that purport to benefit the Canadian soul, in fact undermine it. Wise and skillful discernment is all the more necessary in our age where manufacturing consent is an operation many corporations, governments, and systems use to maintain actions that are ecologically unsustainable and/or socially unjust.

Discernment is important not only for the external arena of social and political action, but also for the internal world of the heart. Learning how to discern the inner movements of one's own heart and the inner motivations for political action is indispensable for those seeking to maintain a spiritual approach to social and political action. Successful actions that promote the *anima mundi* or national soul are important. So too is taking care of one's own soul in the midst of it all. If I wish to bring about a more ecologically sustainable, a more economically just world, or a more inclusive society, I must canvass my interior motivations to ensure that I am guided by love and compassion rather than pride, anger, or resentment. In this case, Thomas Merton's concern for the person and the being of the activist more than the activist's concern with goals rings true.[10] The heart of an activist has just as much, if not more, impact upon others as the change and action pursued. Moreover, I must be prepared to live with the changes that are required of myself as an individual to sustain and embrace the systemic transformation I advocate. I must, as Gandhi advised, bear witness to the change within my own life.

My own experience has been that using and teaching discernment can best take place during a time of brainstorming and analysis of a social/political/ ecological problem in collaboration with quiet, reflection time. When I led the three-day Inner City Retreats mentioned previously, it was important that students not only have hands on learning experiences, but that they also have input from resource people, informed others, and clients/recipients of social services. From this input, students are able to develop a greater understanding of the complexity of most social issues and the vested interests of the various partners. They are also encouraged to develop strategies that will appeal to the good in the other rather than what is lacking. Most people are willing and able to move towards the common good if given concrete ways and means. Finally, we are able, during times of quiet reflection, solitude, and meditation to do an inventory of our emotions and our motivations for being engaged. The altruistic desire to help others is the seed of spirituality that needs to be nurtured into the strengthened heart of a spiritual practitioner.

I have also used examples from the lives of historical and contemporary Canadians who have been advocates of peace and justice (such as: J.S. Woodsworth, Stephen Lewis, Terry Fox, Elijah Harper, Nellie McClung, and Tommy Douglas) to demonstrate that all people who have sought to bring about justice and peace have faced times of failure, disappointment, and setback. They have all faced moments of trial and desolation during which time they have needed to be consoled. Sometimes this consolation has come from others, from subsequent events, or from a deeper place in the soul of the person. Such role models are grounded people who can celebrate victories and accomplishments but who do not place all their hope in their achievements for they have known the other side of engagement, the side of failure and desolation. Beyond their experiences of success or failure lies their awareness of the hidden ground of love, the current of the soul that sustains them throughout their entire life.

Engagement

Once we have listened to the needs of the community and discerned the best actions to nurture the Canadian soul, we need to move towards action. This movement is the phase of active engagement. Now, since this spirituality is a communal spirituality, it follows that the actions will primarily be actions that the community of the classroom or school will undertake. It will be action that aligns the community of the classroom/school with the Canadian soul. Understandably then such actions will require planning, monitoring, cooperation, and assessment.

Because the actions advanced will be supportive of the Canadian soul, which is always vibrant and multifaceted, students who undertake these actions need to be mindful of the resistance they may face. Some of this resistance will be located in the hearts, ignorance or blindness of individuals. Some of it will be located in sectors of Canadian society or regions of the country. Some of it will be located in the international community or the transnational corporations that have a vested interest in stifling the Canadian soul. Students need to be mindful of these realities as they implement their chosen actions and need to recognize that change is normally difficult to embrace at first. They need to be reminded that true and lasting systemic change is the result of the accumulation of many small actions over time.

The engagement moment can be anything from a simple classroom project like tabulating how much water each student uses at home and how this impacts upon Canada's fresh water supply; to traveling to a different region of Canada to establish, nurture and support a cooperative partnership; to working with the poor and disadvantaged in their community; to welcoming new immigrants and fighting exclusion; to being a voice of tolerance for ambiguity. The essential task is for students to take responsibility for what they can at their age. In this way, they learn that they can be active agents of change and agents of healing in the world rather than passive recipients of a given world. Through such engagement, they learn to give expression to their spiritual life.

The altruism and idealism of youth is an appropriate time to initiate students into this path of engaged spirituality. Students need to be given room and encouragement to implement their ideas for creative social and political change. They need to be included and given room to lead. Both the works of the Keilberger brothers and Ryan's Well (founded by Ryan Hreljac) provide good examples of Canadian youth in action. With the support and encouragement of significant adults—teachers, administrators, and parents—students can learn that when they put their ideas into action they can make substantive contributions to the ongoing manifestation of Canada's soul.

At the same time, students need to be prepared for the roadblocks they will face and for the possibility that the chosen action will not necessarily achieve the results they desire. The young especially need to be prepared for defeat and failure as a possible experience along the path of engagement. Knowing how to embrace the limitations of one's efforts, the failure of one's dreams, or even the awareness that one underestimated the level of systemic inertia and resistance to the common good can help one grow in humility, detachment, and enlightenment. Knowing how to accept and embrace setbacks and failures will counteract bitterness and cynicism, which too often result when a person fails to integrate these experiences in a healthy fashion.

Reflection

The final pedagogical moment for engaged spirituality is the moment of reflection, which is an essential moment for it contributes to the development of wisdom. The inner, reflective part of our nature is just as important as the outer, active part. The balance between the inner and the outer, the contemplative and the active, is the goal of engaged spirituality. It is important to facilitate and nurture this reflective, contemplative phase for from our reflection arises the knowledge which feeds wisdom.

An important part of this phase is to pay attention to our emotions. These could be feelings of satisfaction, accomplishment, achievement, or happiness that come when our actions have been fruitful. They could be feelings of sadness, disappointment and discouragement that come when our actions do not bear the hoped-for result. Not every action will bring the results that we envision. Wisdom accumulates as we learn from our accomplishments and our failures over the years.

Some ways to facilitate reflection include: journaling, group discussion, drawing and writing, silent meditation, guided meditation, and of course, silence. In many of these practices silence and solitude are essential ingredients for without the freedom from outward distraction that silence provides we are unable to allow the fullness of the experience of engagement to penetrate our hearts and souls. Without silence and solitude we are unable to fully digest, comprehend, and integrate the experience of social and political action.

The time of reflection is the moment to encourage depth and interiority. It is the time when we let go of our ego desires and needs and allow the voices of the Canadian soul to speak to our personal soul. It is the time of communion and co-natural knowing. It is the time in which we are invited to grow in our personal and national soul remembering always that the soul is manifest in both areas of our life. Hence, the enlargement of the personal soul serves the national soul. Likewise, any growth or magnification of the national soul enhances our personal soul. As we contemplate and reflect we deepen our appreciation for the presence of soul in our lives as Canadians.

These four elements of engaged spirituality (presence, discernment, engagement, and reflection) function together in an ever-progessing spiral of spiritual growth. Each element contributes to the other and they fold back into each other reinforcing the learning over time. The path of spiritual engagement requires all four to be experienced and lived. As a person moves through the different stages of life and follows the fourfold path of engaged spirituality they grow in spiritual maturity and depth. Engaged spirituality brings a person into the soul of the world and brings the soul of the world into the person. Like breathing, it gives and sustains us in life. When engaged spirituality is practiced within a context where the Canadian soul is valued, students grow in their sense of Canadian identity and grow in their ability to contribute to the Canadian soul.

CONCLUSION

The path of engaged spirituality is one that can be followed throughout the various phases of one's life. It is a path that respects the psychological, spiritual and political development of a person as well as the process of consciousness-raising that accompanies learning today. It is a path that is rooted in community and serves the national soul. It is a path that presumes that a person has made a fundamental option for others, an option that can be expressed in, with, and through the Canadian soul as one part of the *anima mundi* that courses across the world.

While journeying along this path, we walk the path of engaged spirituality with the four-fold pedagogy of presence, discernment, engagement, and reflection. Pursued holistically, this pedagogy can easily be applied to across various subjects and grade levels and throughout the life cycle. The success of this approach is depended, however, on the comfort level of the individual teacher in pursing the way of engaged spirituality. This takes us into the area of teacher formation to which we now turn.

NOTES

1. John P. Miller, *Education and the Soul: Toward A Spiritual Curriculum* (Albany, NY: State University of New York Press, 2000), p. 49.

2. Thomas Groome has taken this approach in his work *Educating for Life: A Spiritual Vision for Every Teacher and Parent* (Allen, Texas: Thomas More Press, 1998). Written for a Catholic audience it offers some keen insights into the importance of spiritual education throughout life.

3. Clive Beck, *Learning To Live The Good Life: Values in Adulthood* (Toronto: OISE Press, 1993), pp. 96–97.

4. Diarmuid O'Murchu, *Reclaiming Spirituality: A New Spiritual Framework for Today's World* (New York: Crossroads, 1998).

5. Ibid., pp. 91–92.

6. Matthew Fox, *Creation Spirituality: Liberating Gifts for the Peoples of the Earth* (New York, NY: Harper Collins Publishers, 1991), p. 18.

7. John L. Elias, *Conscientization and Deschooling: Freire's and Illich's Proposals for Reshaping Society* (Philadelphia: The Westminster Press, 1976), pp. 136–143.

8. Bernard Haring, *Free and Faithful in Christ: Moral Theology for Clergy and Laity* (New York, NY: Crossroad Books, 1978), p. 167.

9. For a good analysis of the importance of solidarity and presence as the foundation for effective social action see Susan Evans and Michael Dallaire "God Calling Through Experience: The Church and the Poor" in *Challenging the Conventional: Essays in Honour of Ed Newbery*, edited by Wesley Cragg (Burlington, Ontario: Trinity Press, 1989).

10. Thomas Del Prete, *Thomas Merton and the Education of the Whole Person* (Birmingham, Alabama: Religious Education Press, 1990), p. 110.

Chapter Six

Teacher Formation

Every educator—and I use the term in its widest sense—should constantly ask himself whether he is actually fulfilling his teachings in his own person and in his own life, to the best of his knowledge and with a clear conscience. Psychotherapy has taught us that in the final reckoning it is not knowledge, not technical skill, that has a curative effect, but the personality of the doctor. And it is the same with education: it presupposes self-education.[1]

For many years now, as I have worked as a school chaplain, I have taken the initiative to encourage graduating students to develop some sort of spiritual practice that they can follow into the adult phase of their journey. In addition, I have introduced them to silence, centering meditation, yoga, and mindfulness. I have also shared my own practices. As an adult, I have followed two spiritual disciplines that I have helped me to integrate my active life as a professional educator and chaplain with my inner life of reflection and contemplation. These two spiritual practices are making room for solitude and taking time to walk.

The solitude I have sought and found has taken place frequently during those times when I have gone on retreat. The rhythm of the school year allows for times of lesser engagement and for opportunities to retreat. That being the case, I have made it a regular practice to annually go on a silent retreat. The location for this silent retreat is often a religious retreat centre, a monastery, a cottage, or a campsite in one of Canada's parks. The important ingredient for developing and encouraging my solitude is the atmosphere of silence that is kept in these locations. Free of the distractions of television, radio, and the Internet and from the normal concerns of daily life, I am able to allow myself to rest, which forms the foundation for reflection. Throughout the time of solitude, my introverted self is given the space to recover from my active life and to reflect deeply upon my soul's progress. Whether the retreat is three days or a week, I inevitably emerge refreshed and rejuvenated, ready to return to my busy life.

I have also grown to appreciate the need to tend to my body and so have turned to walking as a natural exercise, one that I can do almost anywhere, anytime. Normally I include a brisk thirty-minute walk in my day. While walking I attend to my breathing, trying to breathe deeply and slowly. This attention to breathing helps to slow the thoughts that swirl through my mind and bring me to a deeper and calmer place. Not only does it provide me with health benefits, it is also a means to release the stress and worries of life. Walking allows me to center upon that which is truly important in life. When entered into with the intention of listening to the life that swirls around me in the world and in my own personal life, I find this time of centering helps me to maintain a balance and equanimity in the face of life's demands.

Over the years, as I have practiced solitude and walking I have come to bring them together. Now, when I walk, I walk as a solitary person to honour the hermetic nature of my introverted personality. My time of walking is my daily retreat, a time that replenishes me for my life of teaching, leading, and ministering. When I go on retreat now I revel in the additional time I have to be out doors, in nature's splendour, exploring the *more* and wonders of the universe. These two spiritual practices, solitude and walking, are integral to my living my spirituality fully engaged. In my observation, every teacher must develop ways and means to maintain their soul that best suits them if they are to not only survive, but also thrive, in the teaching world. Participating mindfully in the arts, or music, or sports can be a simply way to incorporate contemplation into one's life.

Teaching is a rewarding yet demanding profession. It calls for the entire person of the teacher to be intellectually, emotionally, spiritually, communally and physically involved. In addition to requiring a high level of knowledge and skills it requires the integration of the inner, contemplative and the active, creative life of the teacher. Given the degree of personal investment in this occupation we can appreciate that teaching is a vocation.

Our appreciation of teaching as vocation has been in decline in recent times for many reasons. First, we live in a secular age in which there abides a general cultural skepticism regarding anything even remotely verging on the religious and the word vocation still conjures up negative religious connotations. Second, a vocation implies the development of skill, knowledge and experience that is acquired over a long period of time, often a lifetime. In our age, when people are encouraged to expect to have several careers over their working lives, it is no surprise than that our appreciation of choosing a vocation will have diminished. Thirdly, we live in a time when those who work in public professions, like teachers, are denigrated in a society that champions the courage and enterprise of the entrepreneur. Is this not the message behind the saying, "Those who can do; those who can't, teach"? Such a saying reflects a lack of understanding of what exactly is involved in the profession of teaching.

Teaching as a profession has suffered as well because so much of teaching has been reduced to technique and utility, especially in recent years. Reducing teachers to being mere technicians of knowledge (rather than artists of knowledge) is a byproduct of our mainstream educational philosophy, which is deeply embedded in knowledge as instrumental for the acquisition of power. When teaching as a profession is driven by the way of knowing as power it leads to a disconnect from a holistic appreciation of teaching and the heart of the teacher. Thus, when knowledge as service and wisdom (spiritual knowledge) is not integrated into one's life and the practice of teaching, it is easy to relinquish the understanding that teaching is a calling, a vocation. We in the teaching profession have often colluded with the cultural hegemony of knowledge as power and failed to listen to the promptings of our own spirituality as we practice. Thus, we ourselves have contributed to the decline of an appreciation of teaching as a vocation. While there are historical, cultural and philosophical reasons for this declining appreciation we must also accept our personal and professional responsibility for contributing to this decline.

We need to reclaim the use of the word vocation in teaching for I believe that it points to a more comprehensive appreciation of what teaching is all about.

> Vocation refers to a calling and entails firm commitment to the performance of worthwhile activities that are not merely calculated to advance personal career aspirations of fulfilling minimum job expectations. It incorporates a strong ethical dimension, emphasizing an unavoidable necessity of making judgments about what should or should not be done and a readiness to take sides on significant issues... Vocation stresses personal responsibility on the part of the practitioner that cannot be abrogated by technicist prescription and preconceived formulations characterizing a cult of efficiency.[2]

Such an understanding of teaching as a vocation requires that we move beyond the merely intellectual and technical preparation of the person who teaches. It will mean that we begin to move beyond reducing teaching to a set of techniques. We need to reclaim teaching as an art form. Indeed, the best teachers are artists of knowledge and wisdom and through the exercise of their craft they help to prepare students for life. Teacher formation will consequently mean that we need to include the way of spiritual knowing as part of the repertoire of skills and knowledge for practicing this art.

Some have asked, "Are teachers made or born?" I think the answer is yes. Teachers are born with a vocation but that vocation needs to be nurtured and developed. Indeed, teaching at its core involves paying attention to the *more* in life. There is a unifying and soulful dimension to teaching beyond the instrumental and technical approach that is driven by the Western philosophy of techno-rationalism. If we are to continually renew teaching as a profession I believe that we will need to recover the notion of teaching as a vocation. Like all vocations, it will require skill development and knowledge, but essentially the person who is summoned and called to teaching will be one whose being is expressed through the art of teaching. While some teachers will have a strong call and others will have a weak call, both will need to be nurtured and mentored. Understanding teaching as a vocation reconnects and anchors the teacher into the community at large thus minimizing the distancing from the personal that many professions promote.

If a civic spiritual education is to serve as a middle path across secular and faith based systems of education within Canada, the success of following this middle path will hinge upon whether or not we can reclaim the notion of teaching as a vocation as central to teacher preparation. Such a recovery will mean that those readers who consider themselves teachers have been called, summoned, into the frontline of service. It means that this summons, this vocation comes from a place within. This summons will often come through others who see in you the gifts and talents of a teacher and who call you forth to the vocation of teaching. The institutions of society that nurture and affirm this vocation will collaborate in this summoning of the teacher's soul. To teach is to live in fidelity to this vocation. Such a recovery will necessitate several considerations. Let us turn to these now.

SECULAR AND RELIGIOUS INTERSECT

The first consideration is the fact that the vocation of teaching is a vocation that applies to both secular and religious educators. Regardless of which worldview one feels vested in, it is the profession of teaching that cuts across the divisions between secular and religious. That being the case, how do we understand the teacher? If education is the journey of leading out, then we can define teachers as those who lead out. They are those whose function is to "turn the soul"[3] of students towards life and to orient students towards the *anima mundi*. Teachers are turners of the soul. They must themselves be disciples and pilgrims of the soul as it is manifest within their own lives, in the lives of others, and in the events of the world in which they live.

Secular and religious educators share not only a common vocation to turn the soul but also engage in this common vocation in a shared historical location. That is, they both work at the location of the intersection of the sacred and the profane, the religious and the secular precisely because Canada is a mix of both worldviews. In the here and now, the work of education takes place in real schools where it is impossible to maintain complete separations between the secular and religious worldviews. The impact of media, telecommunications, curriculum, and the practical needs of commerce pull the two worlds together and force a dialogue whether we like it or not. To deny this ongoing and continuous interchange of worldview is shortsighted, futile, and ill advised. It would be to ignore the remnants of the religious narratives that have inspired Canadians to date and which continue to influence our nation. It would also be to overlook the ways in which our secular culture provides the container of support for the pursuit of the religious and the spiritual.

The third area where we see the overlap between religious and secular teachers is in our students. That is, the students who come before us each day are coming from a world in which the secular and the religious are at cross pressures.[4] Indeed, the students who sit in the desks and walk the halls carry within them their own life stories of the intersection and intermingling of the many different religious and secular stories that circulate amongst the diverse families and cultures of Canadian society. Generally, our students are living in a nation where the secular and the religious narratives mingle and intersect. It is folly to purport to provide an education that is neutral or value free. Just as religious narratives influence public schools, via these stories being told in the surrounding culture and in the lives of the teachers and students, so too does the secular narrative of our country influence faith-based schools. There is no such thing as a neutral place in education where these stories are completely censored or muted. It is a testimony to the openness and the willingness of Canadians to embrace ambiguity that this sharing of narratives takes place in the everyday life of our schools.

The vocation of teaching in Canada today is one that takes place "at the complicated intersection of the sacred and the secular."[5] It is at this intersection that the soul of Canada is being lived. It is at this intersection that ideological battles are being waged for the hearts and souls of students. It is at this intersection that teachers are standing, bravely seeking to turn the soul of their students to the good in the world. This being the case, it is all the more important that we be clear about our Canadian soul and how to educate for soulful engagement. For if engaged spirituality is to be a middle path between secular and religious schools, it will require that teachers in both streams be formed in this path of spirituality. Indeed, if spirituality in Canadian schools is to be supported and sanctioned in both secular and faith-based streams of education, we will need to pay particular attention to the spiritual formation of Canadian teachers.

FORMATION IN THE TWO WAYS OF KNOWING

Earlier we explored the difference between the two ways of knowing that need to be integrated into a holistic way if we are to proceed with spirituality in Canadian education. We need to supplement the predominating intellectual way of knowing with the spiritual way of knowing. We need to unite the head and the heart into an integral way of learning and teaching so that we can journey forth and engage the currents of the Canadian soul that require our attention. The union of head and heart is a task which teachers themselves must embrace if they are to be able to lead their students along this path.

Most Canadian teachers are already well trained in the intellectual way of knowing. In fact, most teachers have excelled in this area. They have been accepted into teacher colleges and been accredited to teach in our education systems, which are driven by this way of knowing. Moreover, the subject specialization and professionalism that permeate our education systems stand upon this way of knowing. There is much good in it. Pursued singularly, however, it leads to a one-dimensional way of learning and of educating. Moreover, the fixation and reliance upon this one way of knowing leads to a partial sight rather than "wholesight."[6] Wholesight only comes with the integration of our spirituality of knowing into our overall epistemology.

Our teacher training centres need to include the spiritual way of knowing and integrate it into their teacher-formation programs. By training teachers to become more skilled in both ways of knowing, the intellect and the heart, and by encouraging an integration of these two ways, we can prepare teachers who are able and willing to lead and educate for a Canadian style of engaged spirituality that will be responsive to the challenges of our day. We need to take seriously the spiritual formation of Canadian teachers for they have a tremendous impact upon the spiritual life of students.

THE SPIRITUAL LIFE OF TEACHERS

To advocate for the inclusion of spirituality into the formation of teachers as professionals is not to call for another skill or technique that would be added to the already full agenda of teacher pre- and in-service development. To the contrary, it is to build on the essentially spiritual nature of the work of education itself. It is to develop an appreciation for the spiritual within and across our disciplines and within and across our practices. It is to open the teacher as a learner of spirituality, a way of being in the world that is open to the *more*, an openness often mediated through sensory learning. It is to enable teachers to trust their own spiritual intuitions and their own spiritual journeys enough to bring these into their professional practice. Including a Canadian civic, engaged spirituality within our teacher formation programs will require paying attention to what is already happening in our country and our world and listening to the presence of the Canadian soul in both its tranquil and turbulent manifestations. It will require that we align our personal lives and our professional lives with actions and attitudes that serve the Canadian soul through the differing lenses of our various disciplines.

Indeed, the teaching vocation is founded upon the engaged spiritual life. Maria Lichtmann, in her book *The Teacher's Way*, discusses how Thomas Aquinas claimed that teaching was *tradere contemplativa*, which translated means "to share the fruits of contemplation."[7] Accordingly, Aquinas did not see the activity of teaching as being at odds with the quieter life of contemplation. Rather, he saw teaching as a profession in which both action and contemplation were integrated. It is one of the few occupations where the integration of contemplation and action is foundational and for this reason it is to be pursued and valued.

Thomas Aquinas believed that teaching sometimes belongs to the active life and sometimes to the contemplative life. Yet, in moving from contemplation to action in teaching, we do not subtract the contemplative and add the active dimension. Put differently, teaching is not a life of action tempered by occasional moments of reflection, but in the words of Thomas Aquinas, the active life in teaching "proceeds from the fullness of contemplation."[8] The essential point to be grasped is the relationship between the active and the reflective dimensions of the life of teaching. As I have tried to argue throughout, engaged spirituality is an integrating path, one that combines the active dimensions with the reflective dimensions. This applies particularly to the teaching life, for teaching, as a vocation is a professional work that thrives when the active and reflective dimensions of teaching are integrated. Teachers intuitively know the importance of integration. Indeed, the highly valued and contentious issue of preparation time in contract negotiations reveals just how much teachers know that they require time to reflect on their practice, to assess not only the student's performance but their own performance as teachers, and to prepare the strategies and methods that will best achieve the learning entrusted to them as teachers. Without time to breathe, to ponder, and to reflect, the teacher becomes overworked and less effective in the classroom. Transfer this appreciation to the area of spirituality and it is easy to ascent to the wisdom of a balancing of action and reflection in creating a learning environment that honours the way of engaged spirituality.

If Canadian teachers are to embrace teaching for engaged spirituality within a Canadian context, it stands to reason then that they themselves must be living and working from the path of engaged spirituality. That is, they must be involved in actions that promote the Canadian soul in and outside the classroom. In order to model the path of engaged spirituality, they need to be living the pedagogy of presence, discernment, action, and reflection. Only in this way will their students perceive them as credible spiritual leaders and mentors. For example, over the years, as I have deepened in my appreciation and need for walking, I've taken to walking to and from school whenever I can. Partly I do this for my personal wellbeing, but partly I do it for the environment, for one less car on the road reduces carbon emissions. I know that students recognize this small action as one step for change and one way to act for the soul of the world.

There will be resistance to moving towards including the spiritual way of knowing into teaching and to promoting engaged spirituality within the teaching profession across Canada. The reason for this resistance is the fact that the way of knowledge-as-power drives the preparation and formation of teachers today. While there are exceptions,[9] it remains true that we rarely see spirituality promoted within the academy and even less so in professional training programs. Since teaching and learning are essentially spiritual activities, to ignore this dimension is ultimately to shortchange and undermine the educational project within Canada. Perhaps the lack of attention to spirituality within teacher preparation programs is due to the lack of a shared and acceptable understanding of spirituality that both the religious and secular streams of schooling could embrace. Without a unifying and foundational method it is difficult to design courses and professional standards so as to enable spirituality to be brought into the mainstream of teacher professional formation. The reflections offered in this work might, hopefully, contribute to a greater openness to include spirituality within the faculties and ministries of education in the future.

Teachers, by and large, are middle-class professionals who have achieved their status through hard work, deferred gratification, and good luck. Generally, teachers have succeeded in the way of education as it is presently practiced. We are the beneficiaries of the way of knowledge as power and so have a vested interest in maintaining the hegemony of this way. As Mary Jo Leddy says in her book *Radical Gratitude:*

Becoming qualified for jobs such as teaching, medicine, law, consulting, and social services involves a great deal of discipline. Fundamentally, it involves delaying gratification, making sacrifices now for some future benefits. Unlike those who inherit wealth or who are born into generations of poverty, people join the middle class only through effort and stay they only through effort. A middle-class status cannot be inherited or passed on. It is up to each individual to earn his or her way into this class. In sum, this is a class of people defined by discipline and formed through delayed gratification. This is a class of people forged through a sense of the future, people who have made sacrifices because there is a point to it all.[10]

Since teachers are invested in their professional, middle-class status, which is borne along by the way of knowledge as power, learning to attend to the spiritual way of knowing will require a shift of focus. It will require a letting go of the hegemony of rational knowledge so as to provide room for the spiritual way of knowing. Such as shift will require a radical openness to the other way of learning and will require a great deal of trust. Until this shift takes place, the way of engaged spirituality will not open to the teacher.

What would be the motivation for shifting one's personal and professional focus away from knowledge as power to an inclusive approach that balances the head and the heart? Obviously, the motivation for this journey would have to be something more than that which has motivated teachers to work hard so as to enter and stay within the middle class profession. Indeed, I would venture to say that the motivation would come from the benefits of attending to the needs of the Canadian soul. It would come from recognizing that my soul is connected to *others*, to community, to Canada as a nation, and to the *anima mundi*.

Aristotle understood the importance of the middle class for the good of society. According to Aristotle, members of the middle class are in the best position to influence the state because they are free of the ills that often accompany the extremes of poverty and of excessive wealth. "The middle class occupies a position of arbitration between the rich and the poor."[11] Middle-class teachers, then, are in a position to be mentors and teachers of the soul. When they exercise their professional art in such a way that the needs of the entire polis are addressed they can have a tremendous influence upon the nation.

Moreover, teachers, who participate in the turning of the soul to the world, bring forth questions that connect the individual with the collective. When I open myself up to the Canadian soul, I see how I benefit from it and where it needs my active participation so as to grow and magnify. Thus, the features of the Canadian soul (rooted in nature, inclusion, justice, compassion, and compromise) form the conditions for my own flourishing and it is in my best interest to work so as to promote these conditions. This work brings me out of any unnecessary preoccupation with my own needs and can motivate me to be actively responsive to the Canadian soul. I begin to see my personal soul as connected to the national soul and through the national soul, a connection to the soul of the world.

DEVELOPING SPIRITUALLY

Teachers, in order to grow and develop along the path of engaged spirituality, need to practice the fourfold method of engaged spirituality: presence, discernment, engagement, and reflection. They need to practice this method while actively seeking and engaging the *more*, the soul in all its dimensions. This engagement can happen concurrently with the way of knowledge as power and their appropriation of the skills and knowledge for their professional practice. In order to do this they need to keep an eye on the Canadian soul as it is manifested in daily life. Since teachers are normally strong in intellectual knowing they will need to exercise a high degree of intentionality to grow in the spiritual way of knowing. Self-discipline and commitment to an integral path of learning will be necessary attitudes for spiritual development.

Recalling the first step in this method, the teacher will need to be present to at least one of the currents of the Canadian soul. Being present can be motivated by an attraction to a particular current of Canada's soul. Such an attraction may be due to a personal affinity or identification with that current or due to a personal recognition that this current presents a growing edge for the teacher. For example, a teacher may be drawn to pursue the concerns of Canada's natural world and explore the issues of environmental sustainability within Canada. They might meet daily in their classroom the reality of Canadian inclusivity as students from many different cultures and religions mix together. For example, teachers who are firm believers in Canadian justice may feel drawn to amplify this value with their students. Perhaps the teacher is motivated towards compassionate service to those who are less fortunate whether in their local community, or in their provincial or national communities. Finally, a teacher may be needed to assist in mediating disputes across the fields of ideas and values, invoking the Canadian soul through the negotiation of compromise. The point is that there are many ways in which a teacher can be attentive and present to the Canadian soul. Very often the particular current, which the teacher is drawn to resonates with their personal soul. Hence, there can be congruence between the personal and the collective soul, and this congruence can be good. Students need to be exposed to our Canadian soul, but they also need to witness teachers who are living in congruence with their own souls. Such witness can have a lasting impact.

This first step of presence lays the foundation for engaged spirituality. Most of us are already present to some features of the collective Canadian soul. The journey for us all is to expand our attention to include each of the various features of the Canadian soul. There is always a growing edge in our spiritual journey that sometimes requires us to move into those areas that challenge us to grow. We need to ask ourselves several questions. What currents of the Canadian soul do I lack? How do I deal with the turbulent nature of the Canadian soul? How can the various currents be more closely connected? With experience and time we can accumulate a wealth of presence, which then helps to lay a broad foundation in education for Canadian spirituality.

With the eye of the heart present and attentive to a current or two of the Canadian soul, the teacher can then move to the area of discernment. The central question becomes how can I amplify the feature of the soul that I have identified in my personal and professional life? Likewise, what fears, apprehensions or denials of the turbulent side of the soul do I need to become aware of? Moreover, where am I developmentally in terms of my life journey regarding this soul's current? Ultimately, how can I contribute to the beneficence present in the Canadian soul and how can I best educate for this feature of the soul?

As I gather data and bring my critical thinking skills to bear on this current of the soul, I ask myself how internally free I am to deal with this current. For if I am to lead my students to inner freedom, it presupposes that I am free myself. Are there any obstacles to my freely engaging the soul? I follow this with the use of my imagination, thinking of how I can assist in the amplification of the soul today and also what the future ramifications of any action I take might be. Then I listen to my feelings and the promptings of my heart as I entertain my imagination. I use all that I have listened to during my inner scrutiny and discernment to create lesson plans that will bring my students into a learning experience with the soul. I also use all that I have heard during my discernment to deepen my personal presence to the soul's current upon which I have chosen to focus.

After having exercised a degree of presence and moved through discernment to decision, the teacher then moves towards the active phase. The teacher moves towards the delivery of the lesson, which, because the soul is communally conditioned, ought to include communal action. Hence, teachers will look for actions which a group, a class, a grade, or even an entire school can take part in. This active phase will include the teacher's action for the soul as well as the students; for together, they create one learning community and therefore mutually influence each other on this spiritual path.

An example of such action might be an environmental action that students undertake. Building a communal garden in the school yard, challenging homes to decrease their water consumption, increasing the use of walking and bicycling, and even lobbying governments to enact progressive environmental legislation, are all examples of ways to engage the Canadian appreciation of nature. Findings ways to encourage students to pursue economic justice, to raise questions around homelessness and poverty, to lobby governments on behalf of refugees, are ways to engage students in the current of justice. Bringing people of diverse cultures together, visiting different religious churches or cultural centers, and helping to reveal the history behind differences can assist in developing an appreciation for openness. Partnering with non-government organizations, visiting senior centres or hospitals, and participating in food and clothing drives are ways to break open the need for compassion, which is a deeply held Canadian value. Exposing students to the diverse ways of looking at issues in age-appropriate ways can help to build a sense of an appreciation for ambiguity and to practice the art of compromise, which so often characterizes Canadian culture.

Finally, teachers will want to move into the fourth phase of engaged spirituality, that of reflection. Part of this phase will include the ways and means for evaluating the fruits of the action. Such evaluation will not necessarily be on concrete and objective criteria, although it might indeed include these. No, the focus will be more on how the actions feel and resonate. It will include an estimation of the impact, present or future, of the executed action. Do the actions make more evident the current of the Canadian soul that we identified as worthy of our investment of time and energy? Do we feel a deeper sense of belonging, ownership and identity? Did our actions help to mitigate any turbulent elements of the soul? Are we tranquil and peaceful as a result of this action or turbulent and discordant? Questions such as these can help in the evaluation of the action taken.

The reflection is not so much a cognitive and intellectual reflection as a reflection based on attending to the deeper dimension of life, the unity and foundation of the soul in all creation. Thus, listening to the presence or absence of soul in our local context and in our personal life will be the focus here. Essentially the reflective moment will be to know and understand how the reality of the Canadian soul has been magnified through our engagement. From this reflection, teachers will know how to be witnesses to a soulful life while in their classrooms and schools.

Teachers can help facilitate this reflection moment in a number of ways. A key way is to include an appreciation of solitude and silence. In silence, the soul speaks loudly. Indeed, take away the distractions that normally inundate us each day and you may hear a cacophony of voices, some glorious and some not quite so glorious. Over time, as these inner voices grow quiet, one is better able to listen to the depths of one's self and better assess one's inner response to the active work undertaken. Indeed, a key spiritual practice found in all word religions is the need to embrace silence and solitude so as to grow in the spiritual life. Thus, taking time each day to reflect upon one's teaching practice can be a great service to one's spiritual life and ultimately to one's professional practice. Moreover, a teacher who has taken time to listen deeply and quietly to the promptings of the soul will be a teacher who is more available to their students and ultimately more effective in the classroom.

This phase of reflection will also be assisted with different contemplative practices. John Miller has written extensively on the role of meditation in the teaching profession and has shown how using different meditation forms helps to bring equanimity and calm to the teacher.[12] The Center for Contemplative Mind in Society's very instructive Tree of Contemplative Practices (as shown in Figure 6.1) outlines various practices for facilitating awareness and connection that are found in various world religions and in secular society.[13] It is a very useful tool for teachers. Practices such as dialogue, deep listening, journaling, storytelling, centering, and art can all assist in the development of reflection on action.

The phase of reflection can also involve the use of ritual and symbols especially if used within community. World religions have a wealth of data regarding symbols, music, and rituals for marking important learning events of our lives. Teachers working within secular systems will be able to use symbols and rituals as well, but will need to be creative in establishing and using them with their students. Regardless of which sector of Canadian education they inhabit, teachers can creatively use national symbols (such as our flag, the maple leaf, or the beaver) to help give expression to the study of the Canadian soul. To support an appreciation for nature teachers can easily use symbols from nature: such as water, fire, wind, wood, or seeds. Inclusion can be mediated by using circles, roundtables, communal sharing, multicultural and multifaith celebrations. Justice can easily be symbolized through images most often found in our courts, but also through the artists' depiction of the just allocation of goods and services. The visual arts are a well of resources for conveying the value of compassion in Canadian soul. Finally, the experience of compromise is something that could easily be ritualized by simply bringing diverse and contentious partners together to work for and celebrate the common good.

Novice teachers of the way of engaged spirituality may wish to begin to follow this fourfold method with more experienced teachers. They may even seek a support group comprised of a small group of teachers through focus groups or mentoring circles. When I first entered the teaching profession I had the unique opportunity to experience the value of such a group. Once a month a superintendent, a consultant, another high school chaplain and myself met over an extended lunch to share and discuss what was working or not working in our profession practice as spiritual animators. These monthly meetings were times to share experience and to offer support and something that I truly valued. If novice teachers are offered a forum to meet they can become familiar and practiced in the art of spiritual living as they begin to include this method within their teaching practice and with their

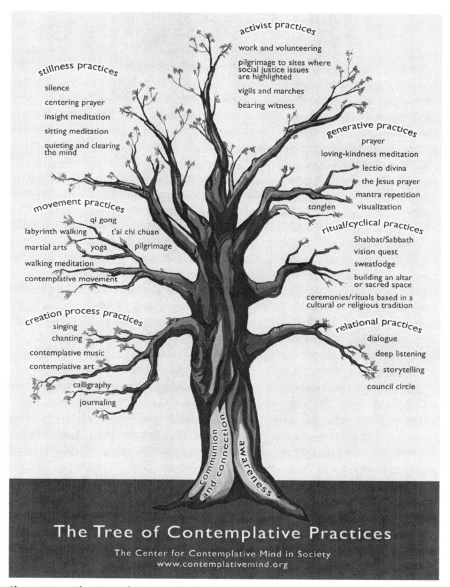

Figure 6.1.   The Tree of Contemplative Practices.

students. There is much wisdom in sharing and learning from one's peers. While teachers do not need to be experts in this field, they do require a certain level of competence so as to be able to be models and leaders for the next generation. In this regard, experienced spiritual teachers can act as mentors and elders to the newer generation of teachers.

THE SPIRITUAL RELATIONSHIP
BETWEEN TEACHER AND STUDENTS

Teachers need to be practitioners of engaged spirituality themselves if they wish to lead students along this path. Indeed, a teacher who pursues the path of engaged spirituality within a Canadian context will be the best model. Such teachers will be able to appreciate and speak about the connections between the various currents of the Canadian soul, be able to point to the hidden ground of the universe that permeates diversity, and be able to differentiate within an historical consciousness between the tranquility and turbulence in the Canadian soul. They will be fluent in the practice of engaged spirituality and be able to guide their students through the method of presence, discernment, action, and interpretation. They will be contemplatives-in-action for a new age, an age that requires the integration of the political and the mystical.

Such teachers will see their professional role as more than simply one of inculcating students into the established Canadian order. They will see their role as a transformative and public spiritual guide able to connect the demands of the national soul with the needs of the personal and individual lives of their students. More than simply being public, transformative spiritual guides, such teachers will see themselves as agents and midwives of a new generation of Canadian citizen, one who is able and willing to engage the challenges of our secular age with spiritual energy and vision. Ultimately, such teachers will teach for an alternative "way of being in the world."[14]

Such teachers will be less concerned with the status quo, and more concerned about creative change. They will focus more on transformation than on conservative banking pedagogies wherein students receive and store data for possible future use.[15] Such conservative pedagogies tend to serve to indoctrinate students into the rule and values of society[16] rather than transformation. The focus of engaged spirituality will be to transform and to magnify the best of the Canadian soul so as to allow it to permeate and enliven our nation. Spiritually engaged teachers will also go beyond the reform stance of liberal educators who, thinking they are critical of society, are too caught up in the myths of progress through social melioration, meritocracy, professionalism, and traditional schooling for their work to be truly radical.[17] They will seek a more personal and comprehensive approach, one that includes the social and political demands of action.

In this regard, the relationship between the teacher and the students will be markedly different from the prevailing cultural one of power and powerlessness. The teacher will not be seen as the one with all the power, nor will the students be seen as the powerless ones who need to learn. The relationship will be more of a partnership. It will be marked by a sense of communion and teamwork. There will be a sense of fellow pilgrims and seekers gathering when the teacher and the students come together to study and to learn from each other how best to spiritually engage the issues facing Canadian society today.

As fellow pilgrims and seekers, teachers and students will often be in different developmental places in their personal lives. There will still be differences due to experiences, age, perspectives, and responsibilities. Sometimes students will have more experience with a dimension of the Canadian soul than the teacher has. These differences will simply fuel the dynamism within the learning experience and make education more of a dynamic experience. When students and teachers embark upon the journey of engaged spirituality together, they can learn from each other and make the journey a truly communal one based on a shared pilgrimage in the life of the Canadian soul.

This dialogical relationship between the teacher and students will help to develop a sense of community in the learning context. There will be a back and forth dialogue between teacher and student as they explore how to engage the Canadian soul in a spiritual way. In this new relationship, both teacher and student know themselves as being continually on the path and continually learning and growing as they follow the path of engaged spirituality throughout their life. A relationship marked by mutual respect and communion would do wonders to renew and transform the classroom experience for both teachers and students. It will help to create inclusive learning communities where the soul, in both its personal and political manifestation, is at the center of teaching and learning.

THE CANADIAN CONTEXT FOR TEACHERS

There is already much within Canada that supports teachers in the development of their spiritual life. Think of the very fact that we live in a country where there is a comparatively high level of peace, security, and prosperity. These conditions help to provide the context for pursuing spiritual questions for we know that if most of one's energy is expended in establishing these conditions, there is little energy left for the spiritual quest. On top of this Canadian teachers are fortunate, by and large, to have easy access to natural habitats in which to explore active presence to the environmental concerns that need addressing. Most teachers can arrange a field trip to a park or outdoor location in which they and their students can be immersed in the joys and concerns of the natural world. Moreover, we live in a country where we have relatively free access to information, an informed and free press, and the rule of law to protect our freedoms.

The Canadian mosaic presents ample opportunity for reflecting upon the value of openness and inclusion. Most certainly, given the growing presence of visible minorities and our burgeoning multifaith reality, particularly in urban centers, we have plenty of opportunities for engaging this feature of Canada. As well, the students who fill our schools today come with their own stories, some familial and cultural, of the experience of being welcomed to

Canada or the struggle for identity and belonging. Wise teachers will know how to work with this raw material of the Canadian soul.

Canadian teachers work in a nation governed by a democratic constitution that includes the rule of law and the Canadian Charter of Rights and Freedoms. This experience not only gives them protection to educate for justice and equality under the law. It also gives them the mandate to awaken within their students a love for justice and peace. While this legal context shapes the often contentious debates regarding what constitutes justice in our society, the truth remains that we are able to debate the differences between communitarian and libertarian notions of justice without fear of reprisal. This ability is a tremendous advantage, for in many places of our world such assurance is not a given. The current of justice will also require that we educate for those parts of our nation that are not reaping the economic benefits of global capitalism. There are many individuals and sectors of our country that are being left behind as the gap between the rich and the poor continues to widen. Teachers, as middle-class professionals, have much that they can offer to bridge this gap and to educate for a society where all are included economically and socially.

Compassion is another attribute of our national soul that is easy to access. Teaching itself, as a work with people, constantly taps the compassion of teachers. Positioned on the frontlines, teachers are often very aware of the needs of their students and their families. Moreover, they are the ones who help students to find practical ways to respond with compassion and sensitivity when tragedy or hardships strike. I've seen this over the years when there is a death in a family, or a fire in the neighborhood, or even natural disasters like the tsunami in Southeast Asia in December of 2005 or the earthquake in Haiti in 2010. Teachers easily respond and engage their students in responding to the needs of their local communities and those in the world at large.

Finally, there is no lack of opportunity for teachers to educate for the Canadian propensity for compromise. Canadian history is full of examples of how compromise served the national identity and soul. Indeed, Canada's lauded reputation as a peacekeeping country is rooted in this feature of the Canadian soul. Compromise is part and parcel of the democratic fibre of Canada, part of our soul, and one that students can easily learn.

The path of spiritually engaging the Canadian soul within education will require an amplification of our concern for the environment, our passion for justice, our openness to the *other*, our compassion for the less fortunate, and our ability to live with compromises on complex moral and legal issues. There is currently some room to explore these currents of the soul within Canadian schools today. Bringing Canadian spiritual education to the forefront will require an activist and political bent to create more opportunities for such education in our schools and the facilitation of engaged spirituality within the teaching profession. This movement will require the leadership at various levels within Canadian education to support the inclusion of spirituality in our schools today. Let us turn our attention now to this important area, the area of educational governance.

NOTES

1. Carl G. Jung, *The Development of Personality: Papers on Child Psychology, Education, and Related Subjects,* trans. R.F.C. Hull (New York: Princeton University Press, 198), p.140.

2. Michael Collins, *Adult Education as Vocation: A Critical Role for the Adult Educator* (London and New York: Routledge, 1991), p.42.

3. Thomas Groome, *Educating For Life: A Spiritual Vision for Every Teacher and Parent* (Allen, Texas: Thomas More Press, 1998), p. 275.

4. Charles Taylor, "Cross Pressures" in *A Secular Age* (Cambridge, MA: The Belknap Press of Harvard University, 2007), pp. 594–617.

5. Parker Palmer, "The Grace of Great Things: Reclaiming the Sacred in Knowing, Teaching, and Learning" in *Holistic Education Review*, Vol. 10, No. 3. (Fall 1997), p. 10.

6. Parker Palmer, *To Know As We Are Known: A Spirituality of Education* (San Francisco: Harper and Row, Publishers, 1983), p. xi.

7. Maria Lichtmann, *The Teacher's Way: Teaching and the Contemplative Life* (Mahway, NJ: Paulist Press, 2005), p. 7.

8. Margret Buchmann, "The Careful Vision: How Practical Is Contemplation in Teaching" in *American Journal of Education*, Vol. 98, No. 1, (November 1989), p. 54.

9. Professor John P. Miller has been offering courses in meditation and contemplation for many years at OISE and has written extensively in this area. He is one of the few who are providing such formation for teachers in Canada today.

10. Mary Jo Leddy, *Radical Gratitude* (Maryknoll, NY: Orbis Press, 2002), pp. 124–125.

11. Aristotle, "Politics" in *Introduction to Contemporary Civilization in the West* (New York: Columbia University Press, 1960), p. 59.

12. John P. Miller, *The Contemplative Practitioner: Meditation in Education and the Professions* (Toronto: OISE Press, 1994).

13. See http://www.contemplativemind.org/practices/tree.html

14. Palmer, *To Know As We Are Known*, p. 30.

15. Paulo Freire, *Pedagogy of the Oppressed*, trans. by Myra Bergman Ramos (New York, NY: Herder and Herder, 1970), p. 58.

16. Henry A. Giroux, *Teachers As Intellectuals: Toward A Critical Pedagogy of Learning*, intro. Paulo Freire, foreword Peter McLaren (Granby, MA: Bergin and Garvey Publishers, 1988), p. 34.

17. Ibid., p. 36.

Chapter Seven

Spiritual Governance

An education system is not the education of this child or this young man
or this young lady. It is a flow of educations. It determines what flows and
the direction in which it will flow.[1]

Few who work within education will deny that there is a political dimension
to schooling. It is true, as Bernard Lonergan has said, that education systems
determine the flow and direction of schooling through what is included or
excluded from the curriculum, to who is and who is not hired, to where the
money flows within the systems. On top of these choices there is the oversight
of government that directs the philosophy of education in the understanding
that education systems are meant to inculcate the young into the mainstream
of society. Under the many layers of governance that oversee the classroom,
the teacher labours, trying to turn the souls of students to the soul of the
world. Most teachers try to keep politics out of the classroom. Not because
they necessarily believe that education can ever be a place of neutrality, but
more because they desire to exercise personal and professional care over their
students. Still, at times the politics of education in Canada impacts upon the
classroom in real and significant ways and teachers respond to protect their
interests and those of their students.

For example, in the autumn of 1998 the political unrest in Ontario between
the provincial government and the Ontario teachers had reached an impasse.
The Progressive Conservative government of Mike Harris planned to implement massive funding cuts to the education sector and to institute stiffer con-
trols over the teaching profession, one of which was to remove administrators
from the teachers' unions. Particularly disturbing were the Draconian methods used by the government and the apparent disdain with which they viewed
the teaching profession. These did little to encourage Ontario teachers to trust

the government, their employer. Teachers, already recovering from the recession of the early nineties and from the educational changes ushered in by the previous NDP government of Bob Rae, were understandably suspicious of any changes to the education sector that did not involve their voice around the table. Indeed, there were signs that change fatigue was settling into the ranks. The disagreements widened and the acrimony intensified until finally all five teacher federations of Ontario agreed to a provincial wide work stoppage. They called on all teachers to stop work so as to boycott the passage of Bill 160 which was the legislation planned to bring in the government's educational agenda. The illegal strike, as the government called it, lasted two weeks and ended when the teachers eventually went back to work despite having failed to stop the government from passing its Bill.

I was working at the time as a chaplain in a suburban school and was hired in a non-unionized position, eventhough I was a certified teacher. Thus, when the teacher federation leaders called on their members to strike I was under no obligation to follow. No threats of retaliation were made by any teacher should I decide to stay in my school and not join the strike for it was understood that this action would be undertaken by unionized staff. However, after a process of deep listening, during which I talked to administrators and teachers, read the actual proposed legislation, and imagined what our schools would look like five to ten years down the road if the legislation passed, I decided to join the teachers in their province-wide strike. In my heart, I could not support a legislative agenda that I believed showed little evidence that it would improve the lives of the most vulnerable students within the school system, which would undermine the professional integrity of teachers, and which would provide the conditions for a more fragmented workplace. I could see little evidence that the withdrawal of hundreds of millions of dollars from a public system of education during a time of increasing enrolment due to immigration, changing demographics, and aging buildings needing repair would be beneficial to students. Moreover, believing that the means must always be as just as the ends, it seemed ill-advised to accept legislation that did not have the support of those who would inevitably have to bear the day-to-day burden of implementation, teachers. For these reasons, I walked in solidarity with the teachers, day after day in their picket lines in the hope of ensuring an education system that would benefit all students and which would promote the sense of informed and responsible citizenship in which I believed. Walking the protest line with fellow educators provided me with an opportunity to listen to the real concerns and stories of everyday teachers, which I felt were not being attended to by the provincial government of the day.

Individual participants of this political protest action will have their own assessment of the legitimacy and efficacy of the action. Few can deny that it had significant impact upon the course of events within Ontario education

that followed. Indeed, the legacy of the protest remains. Historians, in the
not too distant future, will eventually be able to offer greater perspective on
this political action, its context and its consequences. Moreover, Canadian
educators will see in this protest another example of the many times in which
politics and education have clashed throughout the history of Canada. For me,
it was a prime example of when I, as a contemplative-in-action, felt moved
to engage in the area of governance of education, particularly with an eye to
how governance impacts upon the field of spirituality within of education.

SOUL KEEPERS

I have, throughout this book, been drawing out a middle way for spiritual
education; one that goes beyond the two main streams of educational thought
and practice in Canada, the secular and the religious. In a sense this third way
is the spiritual way in which the winds of the Canadian soul are allowed to
knead and influence these two streams with creative and sustaining energy.
Likewise, the secular and the religious ways of being in the world give rise
to thoughts and actions that ultimately impact upon of the soul of Canada.
The reciprocity between the currents of the soul and the streams of thought is
mutually beneficial and something to be cherished and nurtured. The task of
an educator is to facilitate within students the capacity to enter into this dialogical relationship between soul and knowledge so that the student becomes
an active participant in the life of the nation.

I have little managerial or political experience myself, having devoted
myself rather to the paths of teaching and spiritual animation. Consequently,
I have little experience from which to draw upon when it comes to the issues
of management and governance of education. Yet, in my role as a chaplain I
have often been part of the decision-making that takes place within schools
and boards. Sometimes I have been asked privately for my advice; sometimes
I have given it even when not asked. Sometimes I have served on committees
that help to formulate, interpret or execute educational policies. Certainly,
having worked in schools for twenty years, I have seen the impact of policies
upon the daily life of schools and upon the lives of students.

As one who holds the political dimension of life as constitutive of my self-
understanding and who values the importance of institutions for the transmission of knowledge, I do hold some thoughts on the governance of education
in Canada, particularly where it applies to the field of spirituality. Most
importantly, if Canadian educators are to educate for an appreciation for this
beneficial relationship between soul and education, they will need to attend
to the questions of governance. That is, how will access to spiritual education

and the Canadian soul be organized? How will it be protected and cared for? How will the teachings of the soul be evaluated and passed on? How will we design our buildings, or programs, our policies to reflect a spiritual orientation? What conditions regarding schooling itself will be required in order to promote such an education? Finally, how would deliberately including spirituality into our professional practice influence our education systems in Canada? Such questions require that we develop a deeper appreciation of our personal, professional, and collective roles in promoting spirituality within Canadian education. We need to reflect upon how all of us, from teacher to administrator to trustee to politician, are keepers of the soul of Canada.

On the most significant level, the concern for the stewardship or governance of the spiritual within Canadian education relies upon sound, spiritual leadership. Thus, we must attend to the spirituality of leadership, to the attitudes held by those who are vested with systemic and political leadership. A spirituality of leadership speaks to how we lean into the hard questions of collective living and systemic life as an organism. It calls for the development of wisdom, understood as the capacity to sense the good and as opposed to only knowing the good. It calls for the facilitation of right action to accompany right teaching.[2] In this manner, it speaks to how we pay attention, how we discern, how we judge, and how we act to ensure the continuance and growth of the soul that flows across Canada. It speaks to our awareness of how Canada's soul is connected to the world soul. Given this awareness, leadership development within Canadian education requires the development both of the inner person and their skills for keeping alive the soul that flows across Canada today. It requires leaders who are able to call forth the best in schools and in teachers so that the optimum conditions are established to nurture the spiritual life of Canadian children. Moreover, the move towards the area of educational governance demands that we begin the move away from the theoretical considerations to the practical considerations of everyday school life. The development of wisdom (as knowledge married with experience) becomes the way to follow. Wisdom requires not only humility of heart, but also an openness to learn from experience and from others, both of which are essential ingredients to the vocation of teaching.[3]

THE TEACHER AS SOUL KEEPER

The most important person, after parents, for the promotion of civic spirituality within Canadian education is the front-line teacher. That being the case, it is imperative that teachers be soul keepers extraordinaire. They must be able to first pay attention to their own inner life and to their own spirituality. That is, they must be aware of their own unconscious and deeper life and how it is operative within their professional practice. As Carl Jung has warned, if a person is not aware of their inner dynamics, particularly the shadow, they will carry these out in the outer world of action. Parker Palmer has written extensively on this dynamic and argued that the inner life of the teacher needs just as much attention as the outer world of knowledge and technique.[4] The teacher who is able to connect their inner world with their outer world of teaching is an artist rather than a technician. Moreover, the teacher who allows events from the social, political, religious, economic, and ecological realms to inform his or her inner life will become an artist of transformation.

Teachers are responsible for classroom management, for setting the context for learning in the classroom and for establishing the tone and environment in which students may learn. They are the ones who establish the presence in which learning takes place. They are the ones who invite students into this presence. Moreover, they are the ones responsible for introducing students to the way of engaged spirituality in ways that are age appropriate and subject specific. As I have suggested above, there are as many ways of doing this as there are teachers and subjects. Teachers, especially if they work in teams with other professionals, have many ways of teaching students. What is key is that they live and learn the method of engaged spirituality, practice it, and then bear witness to it. The successful transmission of the way of engaged spirituality depends upon the degree to which individual teachers live integrally and congruently both the inner life of reflection and the outer life of action. We are continually growing ourselves along this path of integration and often experience our limitations and our vulnerability. Students, by and large, will respond to the level of experience we have with this path and to the honesty with which we teach. In a sense, teaching spirituality today depends more on the soul and integrity of the teacher than it does on the details and scope of the curriculum.

A teacher must govern his or her own life and practice as the condition for establishing the classroom as a spiritual location of learning. Teachers must take steps to nurture their own spirituality and become familiar with the inner and outer ways of action (and how these two connect). Choosing a practice that helps to deepen their reflective capacity will add in this undertaking. Taking time to retreat from the business of life will also help move a teacher along the spiritual path. Key to such movement will be the corresponding movement of acting for transformative change within the social and political arenas of life. Putting one's heart into communal actions to support the Canadian soul is a necessary ingredient in growing in a civic spirituality. The personal and professional choices that need to be made to support one's growth in the spiritual life need to flow easily from within the heart of one's life. Yet, there will also be times when such choices will require some cost to the personal and professional life. The wisdom of the ages teaches us that at times spiritual growth does cost.

SCHOOL-BASED ADMINISTRATORS
AS SOUL KEEPERS

As important as the classroom teacher is in promoting the spiritual path, it is equally important that school-based administrators be aware of their responsibilities for facilitating the spiritual path. Every teacher knows that much of their success in the classroom is connected to the ways in which they feel supported by their administration. Indeed, schooling is a practicing partnership between the classroom teacher and the school-based administrator. Now, just as each teacher possesses different classroom management styles, so too do school-based administrators. In terms of school governance each principal, vice-principal, department head, or curriculum leader has their own gifts and limitations, which they can use to support front-line teachers in their task of turning the soul of their students.

Support for engaged spirituality in the school goes beyond supporting individual teachers, important as this task may be. Administrators also have the mandate and the responsibility to set the tone for the entire school and thereby create a welcoming climate beyond the individual classroom. For example, administrators know how crucial it is to maintain a safe school so that students will be able to learn. Through their responsibility they often possess a perspective on the whole school that surpasses that of the classroom teacher and this larger perspective of the whole is an important consideration in directing the school in its spiritual life. Moreover, administrators have the local authority to encourage or discourage certain activities. Often, through their access to school-based budgets, they have greater means than the classroom teacher to support school wide activities or directions. In addition to this access, they have direct influence over staffing issues and cooperative partnerships among teachers, other educational workers, as well as parents and the larger community. A wise and experienced administrator can influence greatly the school atmosphere through their judicious and insightful use of talents and resources.

There are various ways in which administrators can encourage engaged spirituality in the school. They can support the formation of school-based clubs that embrace engaged spirituality as core to their identity. At the secondary level, for example, an Amnesty International Youth Group can be a good club for students to learn about ways to engage their passions for justice just as a Multicultural Club can help to honour and celebrate students of different cultures. They can encourage the use of silence and build this into the rhythm of the school day; perhaps begin each day with ten minutes of quiet during which students and teacher can nurture their contemplative dimension. They can incorporate the method of engaged spirituality within staff meetings and professional development days. They can designate physical space in the school, if there is none already designated, for quiet reflection, meditation, mindfulness, and group discernment and create a chapel or quiet room for these purposes. In secular schools such places will be relatively free of explicit religious symbols while in faith-based schools the use of religious symbols will be presumed. In this regard, out of respect for the diversity of religious traditions in Canada today, faith-based schools would demonstrate their hospitality by welcoming persons from other faith traditions into their designated spaces. Finally, since a major component of the path of engaged spirituality will include the natural world it stands to reason that whatever administrators can do to designate and use the outdoor grounds that surround the school for the teaching of sustainable ecological practices would be a good thing. School composting projects, school gardens, recycling programs, energy audits, and advocacy of simpler living can all be easily incorporated into the life of a school.

Both staff and students will respond to initiatives that allow them to pursue the Canadian soul from a perspective of engaged spirituality. Administrators, as leaders in the schools, can do much by their enthusiasm and participation to promote this path. Like teachers, administrators will need to attend to their own inner lives, for students will be affected by the congruence and honesty of administrators just as they are by teachers and other educational workers. Paying attention to one's heart grows more important with each step that one takes away from the classroom and into and up the administrative hierarchy found in our systems of education today. Moreover, administrators, like teachers, will need to be actively engaged in movements or organizations that promote the soul of Canada. I remember fondly one principal who always made a point of joining us for part of our annual Inner City Retreat. Along with the students, he helped out in the soup kitchen and did whatever he was assigned. The students definitely noticed his presence and found his service and participation a validation of their engaged learning retreat.

In addition to the employed members of the school community, the parent community also needs to be brought into a spiritual understanding of education and schooling. At the school level, administrators can achieve a great deal through parent-teacher associations, school council meetings, and public forums to introduce and teach the parent community about the path of engaged spirituality. They will need to clarify how this civil spirituality is both similar to and distinct from the various religious traditions that thrive in Canada. Moreover, the parent community, as a source of varied experiences (many of these religious as well as secular), would be a good resource for magnifying the various currents of the Canadian soul. Including the parental community in the development of a spiritual approach to education would help to pass on the Canadian soul because families often provide much guidance in this area. Indeed, parents and extended families can be deep wells of spiritual wisdom. This inclusive practice needs to be extended to local representatives of business, community, and the arts. These stakeholders have much to contribute to the area of a civic spirituality for the common good within Canada's schools. In fact, students will respond well to artists who give voice to their spiritual longings since music and the arts are valued modes of communication with the young.

SCHOOL BOARD LEADERS AND TRUSTEES AS SOUL KEEPERS

If teachers, educational workers, school-based administrators, parents and community representatives all have a role in the promotion of engaged spirituality, it follows that school board administrators and trustees have a role as well. Indeed, at the senior levels of management, where policy and budgets are struck, the impact of decisions supportive of engaged spirituality can be profound and long lasting. The importance of developing a spiritual outlook increases with one's level of systemic authority for the impacts of decisions are more far reaching when they are relayed and actualized through systems. Hence, it is important that spiritual formation become part of the discourse of board leaders.

Board leaders are vested with many differing portfolios of responsibilities, not the least of which are the facilities for schooling. For example, one can think of the buildings in which education takes place across Canada. In many faith-based schools we see the designation of space for religious services, worship, prayer, and meditation. In some secular education settings, we see space given over for the pursuit of silence and meditation. For example, at OISE at the University of Toronto there was a room designated as a meditation/quiet room. It was available to all and free of any specific religious symbolism. Also, at the University of Victoria there is a lovely interfaith Chapel nestled beside a beautiful garden that was built and is maintained by the university's women's organization. It is a contemplative oasis in the midst of the university life. Students in every school, college and university across Canada could benefit from having a designated space for quiet reflection and mediation.

This space would greatly serve the Canadian project for if our students were to discern, to ponder, and to meditate while they learn and act in ways that are aligned with the Canadian soul we would see a more spiritually equipped citizenry. School board administrators and trustees can work together with school-based administrators to determine how the physical space can be added to or renovated to include this practical dimension.

In order to promote engaged spirituality the structure and schedule of a school life needs to slow down so that more respect is given for the spiritual way of knowing. From my years of spiritual animation, I have come to the conclusion that the hurried pace of schooling does little to assist in the development of a spiritual heart. In fact, hurrying works against it. Given the way our schools are currently run, with clocklike precision and factory-like parceling of time, it is no wonder that our schools struggle to support a spiritual outlook on life. In fact, many of our schools operate in ways that reflect the mechanistic and modern obsession with production and exclude the important appreciation with process. What would it hurt to slow things down, to allow for more time to breathe in between classes, and to permit the opportunity for students and teachers to be more reflective upon their actions? The soul does not move according to linear time but rather moves in keeping with a more fluid approach to time. Hence, we need to find ways to incorporate a sense of time and scheduling that respects an education for the spiritual. When we think of the amount of time that is lost, especially at the secondary and post-secondary levels, for transition between classes, washroom breaks, and assemblies and information sessions, it becomes apparent that many of the minutes required for credit-based learning are not actually met in practice. That being the case, we need to be creative in learning to slow down the day so as to create a school climate that nurtures the spiritual in the everyday.

Moreover, policy makers can do much to encourage civil spirituality by encouraging engagement itself. This requires an appreciation for the learning that takes place outside the classroom and for the learning that takes place through action. Some provinces have already mandated community service hours as a condition for graduation and this is commendable. We have also seen the expansion of cooperative learning courses during which students are placed in a work situation and earn credits. These initiatives point in the direction we need to go. However, recent attempts to encourage civic engagement have been too closely tied to rewards via credit accumulation. Linking service to explicit rewards simply debases the outward thrust of engaged spirituality. The real work of education is to teach students how to understand that their own personal soul is intimately connected to the life of the Canadian soul. The motivation then needs to be intrinsic rather than extrinsic.

Actively engaging the core currents of the Canadian soul into our education system will require that we expose students to areas where they can work for the environment, justice, openness, compassion, and compromise and learn through their activities. In a sense, students would learn the spirit of being Canadian by practicing it throughout their education. In order to enable greater engaged learning, senior administrators and trustees will need to be willing and able to provide in-service for teachers and channel time and resources to engaged learning.

Finally, board administrators and trustees need to learn and practice the discipline of discernment. I have already described discernment as the process of questioning for clarification, assessing one's freedom, imagining the future, and listening to one's feeling responses as one entertains the various choices to be made. System decision makers must be proficient in discernment and also be able to bring the process of discernment to the level of the system.[5] Obviously, at a system level the discernment process becomes more complicated and time consuming. The complexity and time-consumption will be in direct correlation to the importance of the decision to be made. Yet, system leaders will need to ask questions for clarification, assess the system's freedom, imagine the system in the future, and listen for the affective response to the possible scenarios being entertained. Including discernment will require at times that we step back from the normal Robert's Rules of Order and the norm of agenda-setting. It will require a heightening of the political nature of system decisions. If school boards are to align themselves with the *more* and the Canadian soul, then it will be necessary that system leaders not only learn the skills for group discernment, but also give themselves permission to practice discernment as part of the exercise of their vocation of leadership.

These four areas, designated quiet space, appreciating soul time, encouraging engaged learning, and practicing group discernment are simply four examples of ways in which senior level administrators and trustees can exercise their support for including spirituality within Canadian education today. To the extent that these decision makers exercise their stewardship over the delivering of engaged spirituality by creating more space for quiet and meditation, slowing down the school day, validating engaged learning, and modeling discernment they we will see spiritual education grow. On top of these decisions, senior administrators and trustees will need to be cognizant and supportive of the fact that engaged spirituality will often include a political point of view or a political action. They will be called upon to maintain their support as long as the political horizon is in keeping with the key currents of the Canadian soul. Such governance requires the will, the encouragement, and the imagination of board leadership and will presume their commitment to the common good.

FACULTIES OF EDUCATION AND
COLLEGES OF TEACHERS

Turning to the levels of professional training and accreditation we see that there is a need for creative imagination if teachers' exposure to the way of engaged spirituality is to be encouraged and sustained. Currently, there are very few faculties of education that provide for training in spirituality.[6] There is a need to include training in spirituality in the various faculties of education across Canada. This change will require recruiting faculty capable of teaching spirituality in non-sectarian and inter-disciplinary ways as well as an appreciation for the socio-political horizon of action required for our times.[7] It will require channeling resources to the writing of textbooks, the running of engaged learning retreats, and the creation of teaching aids to assist in the integration of spirituality as a common thread throughout the full range of teacher training. It will require creating spiritual spaces on campuses where student teachers can practice meditation, mindfulness, and reflection. It will require openness to an appreciation of the need for less structure and more fluidity in teacher preparation programs. Finally, it will require creating retreat experiences that provide the context for the deepening of the appreciation of the soul of Canada and how to transmit this appreciation to others.

The path that I am proposing, the path of engaged spirituality, a path that both religious and secular educators will be able to embrace, will be met with resistance. Part of this resistance will be to including training and accreditation in this path within faculties of education and Colleges of Teachers across Canada. Some resistance may be lead by those who are stridently secular and anti-religious, wanting to purge any semblance of religion from the public sphere. Some secular adherents may fear that any approach to spirituality is simply a back door to religious indoctrination. Moreover, some religious educators will resist this approach to spiritual education because of their fear of diminishing the distinctiveness of their particular religious spirituality. I have tried to argue throughout, such concerns, while somewhat legitimate, are tangential to the ultimate concern of Canadian educators, which is to assist in turning the soul of students to hopeful engagement in the Canadian soul which, with climate change, the widening of the gap between rich and poor, growing social fragmentation and ethical polarization, requires a pedagogy that brings the social and political into the personal and the mystical in ways that speak to the emerging generation of Canadians.

Nonetheless, the concerns of strident secularists and religious deserve a response. Clive Beck, in *Better Schools: A Values Perspective,* has put forth a clear case for incorporating spirituality in schools in such a way that avoids the indoctrinating approaches so feared by secular humanists and the homogenizing toleration feared by ardent religious. Beck states that the negative and pejorative connotation of indoctrination can be applied to both the content of indoctrination and the method of indoctrination. That is, certain dogmas or truths that are taught but don't stand up to reason would be considered negative indoctrination. Also, if such truths are taught in such a manner that students are unable or psychologically unwilling to re-examine the taught content at a latter date, then this amounts to a negative indoctrinating method.

Having stated these reservations, Beck is nonetheless clear that there can be positive functions to indoctrination. Thus, if content helps to initiate a person into a community's myths and traditions, then there can be positive value to it. Likewise, if the teaching is presented in such a way as to allow the student to re-visit and revise the content in light of later learning and maturity, then this presentation is a positive form of indoctrination. One might see positive indoctrination as the quintessential form of education, which is to lead the soul out into the world.

Beck applies his understanding of indoctrination to both religious and secular schools. He is aware that secularism can have its own forms of indoctrination just as religious schools. For example, the scientific method can be used in a negative indoctrinating way if other ways of knowing and other questions are forbidden. Any secular education that denies or dismisses outright the contribution of religious traditions would be guilty of negative indoctrination.[8] Likewise, faith-based education runs the risk of negative indoctrination if it excludes the insights of secular science and the critique of humanists. Beck's clarification regarding the negative and positive functions of indoctrination is very helpful in our consideration of spiritual education within Canadian schools.

One of the major ways that Beck sees we can proceed to avoid the negative forms of indoctrination is to educate teachers on how to identity bias. Moving from the understanding that we all have biases, Beck argues that we need to become more aware of how religious, sexual, cultural, and class bias informs our teaching and our practice. By becoming more aware of the biases that operate, we can more easily and clearly teach students to identify for themselves the issues and concerns, which they will choose to accept and to follow.[9] Raising teachers' consciousness about the impact of bias applies to group bias as well as individual bias.[10] The teaching of consciousness of bias is something which ought to be included within teacher preparation programs across the country and especially if spirituality is included within initial and ongoing formation.

I think that reasonable persons, attentive to the needs of Canadian society and appreciative of the need to include the spiritual dimension in education, could develop training programs and accreditation criteria that would ensure the principles of non-indoctrination and national standards for teaching. This task would require the development of pre-service and in-service courses for teachers, following the method of presence, discernment, action, and reflection that I have outlined above. Moreover, provincial colleges of teachers would need to broaden their own understanding to include a mandate for spirituality within Canadian education. The possibilities are wide open. What will be required is a willingness to put aside our resistance to the inclusion of spirituality in Canadian education and to turn our creativity to establishing the best practices in teacher preparation to facilitate the inclusion of engaged spirituality within Canadian education.

PROVINCIAL AND FEDERAL GOVERNANCE

The inclusion of this approach to spirituality within Canada's professional teacher training programs and accreditation will require the direction of provincial ministries of education. It will require legislation to ensure that each province has faculties of education that offer training in Canadian engaged spirituality and that each provincial accreditation body oversees the provision and certification of teachers in this area. As difficult as this may be for the area of spirituality, I do believe that some level of spiritual governance or oversight needs to be exercised.

One way of providing for this is to appoint a person within the various provincial ministries of education as responsible for the spirituality portfolio. Is it so far of a leap to include the area of spirituality as a constitutive part of Canadian identity and hence concern? There could be a council of Canadian spiritual advisors who give input into the curriculum development and teacher training. Such councils could be struck within each province thus providing ways for local expressions of Canadian spirituality to be included within provincially run schools. Councilors would be elected from various religious groups and secular organizations as well as community, business and political groups. There would be representation from First Nations on each council. These councils would be provincially situated thereby better able to reflect the regional diversity of Canada.

Finally, in the area of spiritual governance, we have the tangled web of provincial and federal levels of government. The division between provincial and federal powers provides the biggest political obstacle for promoting a Canada-wide approach to Canadian engaged spirituality. The founders of our nation could not have envisioned as situation in which the religious worldviews would be so sidelined from the center of civic life and so often contested with a prevailing secular worldview. Nor could they have foreseen the emergence of a multifaith Canadian population within a secular framework. They could not have foreseen a situation in which we would be bereft of the tools necessary to engaged in a public and respectful conversation about the *more* in life, a conversation that spiritual education advances. On top of these considerations, the founders of Canada were dealing with a different degree of regional and political diversity than what we experience today within Canada. In fact, the founders of Canada worked within a very different social, religious and political situation. Yet the very fact that they approached education with a set of philosophical presumptions that included an appreciation for education in the soul supports the development of education for a civil and engaged spirituality that would be in keeping with the Canadian soul.

The reality is that education is the constitutional responsibility of the provincial and territorial governments. The federal government has no direct central or overall responsibility or jurisdiction for education apart from the funding of post-secondary institutions of learning. This does not mean that there are no national bodies seeking to influence the practice of education across Canada and to promote a national perspective. There are, for examples, the pan-Canadian Council of Ministers of Education and organizations like the Canadian Education Association and the Canadian Council on Learning. Influential as they may be, however, they do not have the legislative power to mandate the teaching of engaged spirituality across Canada. They can encourage it, and one certainly hopes that they would. However, supporting and encouraging are a far cry from mandating and enacting. Perhaps the Federal Government could provide leadership by establishing an Office of Inter-Provincial Education, whose mandate would be to oversee and encourage Canada-wide standards for education, including the teaching of civic spirituality.

Including civic spirituality in education can be done in such as way as to enhance our Canadian education system. This would ultimately serve both purely secular and faith-based systems of education by providing a larger framework in which to work. Nonetheless, both of these systems will want to carry out the mandate to educate for civic spirituality according to their own philosophical frameworks. If funding of the system comes from the public purse, then it would be reasonable to expect that each system carry out an education for civic spirituality in ways that are in line with provincial and federal directives. There would need to be oversight of this educational thrust. Each system, under the governing principle of subsidiary, would be responsible for implementing the curriculum in the ways that suit their specific philosophy. The interchange between central oversight and subsidiary application would provide a governing method to provide for spirituality in all Canadian schools.

GOVERNANCE AND FINANCES

One final area for consideration is that of the area of school finances. Education budgets are highly political instruments, full of contention and vision. Through our budgeting we provide direction, we enable, and we shape the direction of educational practice. I am reminded here of Sister Clare Fitzgerald's saying, "Show me your budget and I'll tell you what your mission is."[11] Clearly where you allocate your money indicates what it is that you value.

Given her insight, we need to be mindful that if our education budgets are devoid of money and staffing for the promotion of engaged spirituality, then we can conclude that it is not considered part of the mission. Moreover, if neither physical space nor time is permitted for facilitating spirituality within Canadian schools, we can conclude that it is not a priority. In order to overcome these potential omissions and lacks, it is imperative that teachers, administrators, trustees and politicians find ways to creatively provide for the money required to offer credible programs in spiritual education. If the accrediting bodies in different provinces oversee the operation of such programs then there would be a way to provide accountability for the money spent. Moreover, space in schools for chapels, spiritual rooms, and meditation rooms would need to be included. The critical question will be whether or not politicians and administrators support and believe in the possibilities of educating for a civic spirituality within Canada. Ultimately, their budgets will reveal their answers.

CONCLUSION

There is no doubt that the path of spiritual education that I am advancing will require a paradigm shift among Canadians. In particular, it will require a shift in the consciousness of Canadian parents, educators, administrators, and politicians away from a disregard for the spiritual towards attentiveness to this important dimension in Canadian life. In addition to the development of consciousness and a change in paradigm, there is a need to move towards reflective and disciplined policy decisions in the area of educational administration and governance. It will require that we bring the concern for the soul of Canada and for the path of engaged spirituality into our governance practices. Given that the multicultural and multifaith fabric of Canadian society is growing, it seems only wise to include spirituality in a non-sectarian and socially responsive fashion. Indeed, an engaged, civic spirituality can be a thread of meaning that can help to hold the Canadian tapestry together. To achieve this spirituality, we all need to take our responsibilities for the wind of the soul that flows across this beautiful land and choose to govern with wisdom and foresight.

NOTES

1. Bernard Lonergan, *Collected Works of Bernard Lonergan: Topics in Education—The Cincinnati Lectures of 1959 on the Philosophy of Education*, edited by Robert M. Doran (Toronto: University of Toronto Press, 1993), p. 34.

2. In theological terms 'right action' is often called orthopraxis while 'right teaching' is called orthodoxy.

3. For a fine descriptive and analytical work on the way of wisdom see Jonas Barciauskas, *Landscapes of Wisdom: In Search of A Spirituality of Knowing* (Lanham, New York, Oxford: University Press of America, 2000).

4. Parker Palmer, *The Courage to Teach: Exploring the Inner Landscape of a Teacher's Life* (San Francisco: Jossey-Bass Publishers, 1998).

5. For a discussion of the role of discernment in public policy context see "Public Policy and Christian Discernment" by Thomas E. Clarke in *Personal Values in Public Policy: Conversations on Government Decision-Making*, edited by John C. Haughey, SJ. (New York, NY: Paulist Press, 1979), pp. 212–242.

6. Some graduate level courses are provided in holistic and spiritual studies at the Ontario Institute for Studies in Education at the University of Toronto. But, such opportunities are rare at pre-service faculties in Canada. In the United States, there is the Masters in Contemplative Studies at Naropa University, a Buddhist centered university.

7. Professor John P. Miller at OISE at U. of T. is an example of a person who has provided leadership already in this area. He has published widely around the need to include meditation and other spiritual practices within teacher preparation programs. For example see his work *The Contemplative Practitioner: Meditation in Education and the Professions* (Toronto: OISE Press, 1994).

8. Clive Beck, *Better Schools: A Values Perspective* (Great Britain: The Falmer Press, 1990), pp. 73–83.

9. Ibid., pp. 85–95, 105–116, 129–139.

10. For a good discussion of individual, group and cultural bias see Bernard Lonergan, *Method in Theology* (New York: The Seabury Press, 1972), pp. 53, 217, 240, 270.

11. Sister Clare Fitzgerald, keynote speaker at Ottawa Catholic School Board professional development day, November 1998.

Conclusion:
Teaching with the Wind

In the purity of the morning, I understand how much more there is to the world than meets the eye. I see that the world fails to dissolve at the edges into myth and dream, only because it wills it not to. Now I begin to understand the meaning of that vision. Now I see the truth of it.[1]

After my initial years in the teaching profession I was beginning to have second thoughts about my vocation as an educator. The idealism of my novice teaching years was wearing off as I met the daily reality of being a teacher. I had begun to master the minutia of classroom life and to find my own comfort zone regarding my presence in the classroom. The days were long, but I thoroughly enjoyed being in front of a class of students and felt honored to be a teacher. Yet, the downloading of society's expectations upon the classroom was increasing at the same that money for necessary services was being withdrawn from the education system. On top of this the profession was becoming more technologically driven and a sense of depersonalization was creeping into the schools. I began to lose my bearings and wondered if I was in the right field of work.

I decided I needed to talk to someone about the state of education today and so contacted a director of education in Ontario whom I had met once before. He had impressed me as someone with integrity, intelligence, and compassion. I called him up, and he readily agreed to meet. I took a personal leave day and drove for two hours and arrived at his office shortly before 9:00 a.m. expecting to have a half hour with this busy man. I went in and began to discuss my concerns about the state of education with this director. He was very welcoming and interested, and we talked for three hours!

The bulk of the conversation pertained to the need for a clarification of our philosophy of education so as to be clear about what we are doing when we

147

claim to educate. He appreciated my inquiring spirit and encouraged me to follow my questions, which I did, eventually going on to complete doctoral studies in the philosophy of education. Beyond this encouragement, there are two things I remember from this meeting. First, I was definitely impressed by the fact that this man, who was a busy director of education, would take three hours to listen to a neophyte's concerns and to encourage me. I remember he never once took a phone call while we were there. When the phone did ring he simply said, "Let it ring, you are more important." I learned from him that it is important to spend time with people and to truly listen so that they feel that they are the utmost priority. I have tried to incorporate this practice into my work as a teacher and a chaplain over the years. It is a practice through which I can exercise discretionary control over the intrusion of technology upon the personal, relational dimension of life.

The second thing I remember was that he emphatically stated that, "You must find kindred spirits in the profession!" He claimed that there were kindred spirits who were asking questions similar to mine. There may not be many, but they were there, he assured me. He said that without kindred spirits we cannot keep our own spirits alive and that the demands of the profession would eventually squelch my spirit. I came away from that meeting instructed in this truth and have ever since sought out kindred spirits, people who are asking questions about what it means to be a teacher and seeking the *more* in the midst of teaching. My kindred spirits are teachers who lean into the deeper questions of educational practice and who seek to bring the realm of the soul into teaching. Moreover, they are teachers who see the importance of the economic, social, and political dimensions of life, particularly as these affect the experience of the common good.

We all need kindred spirits. This need is especially true if we are Canadian teachers who are seeking to live spiritually within our profession. We are living in a secular age where religious narratives are sidelined within an homogenizing culture of secular capitalism and yet the longing for the *more*, the ineffable and the mysterious so often nurtured by religion lingers and persists within people's hearts. Indeed, people are searching for life with depth and meaning within secular culture. Our secular valuing of successful action and our cult of achievement has yet to adequately integrate the inner, deeper pursuit of the *more* with the outer, global pursuit of justice, peace, and sustainability. In the secularized West we are longing for a new way, one that reconnects with the spiritual roots of our civilization but also moves within a secular and pluralist framework. In this new and transitional time, when the new has not yet been born out of the old, we struggle to find the language and the form to give shape and expression to a new, yet historically rooted, spirituality. Such spirituality may perhaps be more civil than religious. It is all the more important therefore that those kindred spirits who have their fingers on the pulse of the spiritual within Canadian education find each other.

There are many kindred teachers on the periphery of Canadian education working away in their classrooms or in their offices seeking to live with integrity and holism the spiritual questions of their lives. Some are living in the midst of our secular culture as persons informed by a religious horizon of meaning. Informed by their specific religious teachings, they seek to live the essence of those teachings from their own heart and to bring these teachings forward into the world as it is. Not with a sense of condemning or converting the *other* to their particular religious worldview, but rather with a sense of dialogue and seeking the *more* as it is found in the realities of everyday life. Such an orientation moves the person beyond their religion without denying their religion, leaving the person free to experience the new *more* in the world. Sometimes such an orientation will bring one to the periphery of one's religious community and one might feel as marginalized from one's religion as one feels marginalized from the surrounding culture.

Other kindred spirits are found in those who are not rooted in any particular religious tradition and who identify themselves as secular humanists. They may be atheist or agnostic and yet humble enough to acknowledge the limits of their own horizon of secularism. Such individuals may identify more with the prevailing teachings of secularism in Canadian culture and yet seek the *more* beyond the limits of secularism. They experience in their personal life inklings of the ineffable and the mysterious and yet do not automatically use theistic images or language to express these experiences. They often turn to artists and musicians to give voice to their experiences of the *more*.

Teachers who seek the *more* beyond the limits of the religious and the secular are people seeking the soul in all its dimensions. They do so in the gaps between religion and secular culture, in the primal experiences of life, and in the everyday exchange between people who live and breathe across the land. This place of gaps, the place in between, beyond the borders, is the liminal place. A liminal place is a place of transformation. It is a place where the old no longer suffices, and the new is not yet born. To be in a liminal space is to live with a deep sense of the *more* and yet to be cognizant of the ambiguity present in that space. In the liminal space, one may experience happiness and confidence but also emptiness and anxiety. It is the place where creativity percolates until a new synthesis is born. Even when a new synthesis is given one carries it with the awareness that it is not complete and that we must carry it carefully.[2] Teachers in the liminal place allow the *more* to live as it wishes, not as they wish it to live. Such a place is the life of the soul. It calls us to a deep self-awareness, and it calls us to teach with a deeper appreciation of the soul in life.

Liminality not only applies to a space in an individual's journey. It also applies to the journey of a community or a people. It applies to a time of change and transformation, a historical period in which the old is giving over to the new, a new that is not yet known. Canada has been passing through such a liminal period. The historical expressions of our national soul are being given new life by the changing circumstances of our history. The challenges of globalization, multiculturalism, science and technology, the environment, and human rights are having an impact upon the soul of Canada. A new synthesis of the Canadian soul is percolating and yet it is not ready to be born. When it does it will be incomplete as most manifestations of the soul are. Perhaps it will be as fluid and as transparent as the wind. It will carry with it the energy to inspire Canadians and to help to shape a home of meaning for all who gather across our land.

We might also envision that a renewal of the Canadian soul will include a more deliberate attentiveness to the "why of Canada."[3] If there is a reason for the existence of Canada within our global world, surely that reason will flow from our soul. As a middle power with an empire as our closest neighbour, our global presence will necessarily be influenced by the geo-politics of others. Nonetheless, as a nation forged between European conservative roots and revolutionary republics, our historical experiment with social democracy in a secular age has prepared us to be a model in our postmodern global world. Our ability to hold together the innate tensions that come with the diversity of cultures and religions within a cohesive social project is something to be cherished and proudly proclaimed. Despite the difficulties associated with our geographic and ideological regionalism Canada nonetheless stands as a safe home for many from around the world. Our experience with compromise and the middle way in terms of politics allows us to be a diplomatic resource for our world today. The why of Canada is connected, then, to the world in which we now live.

Given the changing and maturing nature of the Canadian soul, it is clear that our social institutions will be changing and maturing. Education, as one such institution, will need to align itself with these changes. This realignment will require the reawakening of our spiritual nature and a renewal of Canadian education for our spiritual nature. The highlighting of the Canadian soul needs to be matched by a recovery of an appreciation for spiritual education in a way that is in line with a reconstructive postmodern philosophy. It requires a method that moves beyond endless critique to hopeful imagination. Such an imagination will be one that incorporates the historical values of the Canadian soul into the project of the future.

Central to this renewal of Canadian education are our teachers. Therefore it is essential that Canadian teachers be spiritual leaders in our schools. As public artists of the national soul teachers need to bring what they know and continue to learn about the Canadian soul to the center of the classroom. They need to engage in public and professional discourse on the ways and means to include spirituality in our schools so that emerging generations of Canadians are taught how to engage the soul of the nation in life giving ways. Such a discourse must transcend regional differences but not ignore them. It must move us into the future but in fidelity to our past. It must call us beyond the silos of religious and secular education systems. It must focus on the *more* and the common good that keeps our nation together. Such a discourse needs to take place at all levels of Canadian education, from the classroom to the boards of education to the offices of the ministers of education.

Educating for a civic and engaged spirituality within Canadian schools does not mean that we need to eliminate secular and faith-based school systems: quite the contrary. Beyond the limits on both worldviews lies the life of the soul in both its personal and collective dimensions. Both systems offer distinct ways of living in fidelity to the soul. The ways and means through which each system encourages the development of both the individual and the national soul need to be supported and strengthened, for these can only add to our civic and engaged spirituality. Anything that detracts from the building up of our Canadian soul needs to be curtailed. The monitoring of our national soul needs to fall to the area of governance, which then brings education back into the political sphere. Ultimately, it is up to our politicians and leaders to find ways that support and encourage secular and faith-based schools to continue to exist and to serve the common good. My hope is that some of the insights offered in these pages can help in this important work.

Some may say that what I have proposed is an impossible dream and that a national civic and engaged spirituality is impossible. To them, I would respond that there is already much in place to encourage bringing spirituality into our Canadian schools. Indeed, we need not wait until we have it all together, neatly packaged in tight curriculum with uniform standards and with clear political direction. The life of the soul does not respond to tightness and uniformity. Constraints stifle the soul. The teaching of spirituality in Canadian schools must flow from the experience of how "much more there is to the world than meets the eye" as Sharon Butala says. Canadian educators already know this *more* and many already teach from the *more*. We must push our teaching to the edges of our myths and our dreams and allow ourselves to be drawn into the *more* that flows across our great land.

When we accept that we do not have all the answers and that there is more to life than meets the eye, then there is room for the soul to work. To be a spiritual educator is ultimately not to provide all the answers but to help students to ask the correct questions and to set them upon the soul's path. The most crucial questions in life are those of the soul and so teaching, as the art of turning the soul to the world, needs to be learning to live a life for others with deeper questions always held within our vision. When the heart and the classroom are opened up to such searching, there is room for the wind to blow, fluid and unencumbered. This is what it means to teach with the wind.

NOTES

1. Sharon Butala, *The Perfection of the Morning: An Apprenticeship in Nature* (Toronto: Harper Perennial, 1994), p. 191.

2. Diarmuid O'Murchu, *Quantum Theology: Spiritual Implications of the New Physics* (New York: Crossroad Publishing Company, 1998), pp. 161–162.

3. Andrew Coyne, "All is not well in Canada. Don't shrug." in *MacLean's* (April 14th, 2008).

Bibliography

Aristotle. "Politics" in *Introduction to Contemporary Civilization in the West*. New York: Columbia University Press, 1960.

Attenborough, Richard. *The Words of Gandhi*. New York, NY: Newmarket Press, 1982.

Barciauskas, Jonas. *Landscapes of Wisdom: In Search of a Spirituality of Knowing*. Lanham, New York, Oxford: University Press of America, 2000.

Beck, Clive. *Better Schools: A Values Perspective*. New York, NY: The Falmer Press, 1990.

_____. "Education for Spirituality" in *Interchange: A Quarterly Review of Education*. Vol. 17, No. 2, Summer 1986.

_____. *Learning to Live the Good Life: Values in Adulthood*. Toronto: OISE Press, 1993.

Berry, Thomas. *The Dream of the Earth*. San Francisco: Sierra Club Books, 1988.

Bosacki, Sandra Leanne. "Theory of Mind and Education: Toward a Dialogical Curriculum" in *Holistic Education Review*. Vol. 10, No. 3, Autumn 1997.

Boyd, Dwight. "Dominance Concealed through Diversity: Implications of Inadequate Perspectives on Cultural Pluralism" in *Harvard Educational Review*. Vol. 66, No. 3, Fall 1996.

Brown, Robert McAfee. *Spirituality and Liberation: Overcoming the Great Fallacy*. Louisville, Kentucky: The Westminster Press, 1988.

Buchmann, Margret. "The Careful Vision: How Practical is Contemplation in Teaching" in *American Journal of Education*. Vol. 98, No. 1, November 1989.

Butala, Sharon. *The Perfection of the Morning: An Apprenticeship in Nature*. Toronto: HarperCollins, 1994.

Butkus, Russell A. "Linking Social Analysis With Curriculum Development: Insights From Paulo Freire" in *The Journal of Religious Education*. Vol. 84, No. 4, Fall 1989.

Callan, Eamonn. "Pluralism and Civic Education" in *Studies in Philosophy and Education*. Vol. 11, 1991.

Carr, Anne E. *A Search for Wisdom and Spirit: Thomas Merton's Theology of the Self.* Notre Dame, Indiana: University of Notre Dame Press, 1988.

Clarke, Thomas E. "Public Policy and Christian Discernment" in *Personal Values in Public Policy: Conversations on Government Decision Making.* Ed. John C. Haughey S.J. New York, NY: Paulist Press, 1979.

Coleman, John A. and William F. Ryan. *Globalization and Catholic Social Thought: Present Crisis, Future Hope.* Ottawa, Ontario: Novalis, 2005.

Collins, Michael. *Adult Education as Vocation: A Critical Role for the Adult Educator.* London and New York: Routledge, 1991.

Coyne, Andrew. "All is not well in Canada. Don't shrug." *MacLean's.* April 14th, 2008.

Dallaire, Michael. *Contemplation in Liberation: A Method for Spiritual Education in the Schools.* Lewiston, NY: Edwin Mellen Press, 2001.

Del Prete, Thomas. *Thomas Merton and the Education of the Whole Person.* Birmingham, Alabama: Religious Education Press, 1990.

Dillard, Annie. *Pilgrim at Tinker Creek.* New York, NY: Harper and Row, Publishers, Inc., 1985.

Dyckman, Katherine Marie, S.N.J.M. and L. Patrick Carroll, S.J. *Inviting the Mystic, Supporting the Prophet: An Introduction to Spiritual Direction.* Ramsey, N.J.: Paulist Press, 1981.

Egan, Kieran. *Imagination in Teaching and Learning: The Middle School Years.* London, Ontario: The Althouse Press, 1992.

Elias, John L. *Conscientization and Deschooling: Freire's and Illich's Proposals for Reshaping Society.* Philadelphia: The Westminster Press, 1976.

Emberley, Peter C. and Waller R. Newell. *Bankrupt Education: The Decline of Liberal Education in Canada.* Toronto: University of Toronto Press, 1994.

Evans, Susan and Michael Dallaire. "God Calling Through Experience: The Church and the Poor" in *Challenging the Conventional: Essays in Honour of Ed Newbery.* Eds. Wesley Cragg, Laurent Larouche and Getrude Jaron Lewis. Burlington, Ontario: Trinity Press, 1989.

Foucault, Michel. *The Hermeneutics of the Subject: Lectures at the College de France 1981–1982.* New York, NY: Picador Press, 2001.

Frankl, Viktor E. *Man's Search for Ultimate Meaning.* Cambridge, Massachusetts: Perseus Publishing, 2000.

Freire, Paulo. *Pedagogy of the Oppressed.* trans. Myra Bergman Ramos. New York, NY: Herder and Herder, 1970.

Fox, Matthew. *Creation Spirituality: Liberating Gifts for the Peoples of the Earth.* New York: Harper Collins Publishers, 1991.

Galbraith, John Kenneth. *The Culture of Contentment.* Boston: Houghton Mifflin Company, 1992.

Giroux, Henry A. *Teachers As Intellectuals: Toward A Critical Pedagogy of Learning.* Intro. Paulo Freire, foreword Peter McLaren. Granby, MA: Bergin and Garvey Publishers, 1988.

_____. "Teachers, Public Life and Curriculum Reform" in *Peabody Journal of Education.* Vol. 69, No. 3, Spring 1994.

Glazer, Steven. *The Heart of Learning: Spirituality in Education*. New York, NY: Penguin Putnam Inc., 1999.

Gouvernement du Québec: Ministère de l'Education, du Loisir et du Sport. *Developing the Inner Life and Changing The World: The Spiritual Care and Guidance and Community Involvement Service, A Complementary Educational Service*, 2006.

Griffin, David Ray, editor. *Spirituality and Society: Postmodern Visions*. Albany, NY: State University of New York Press, 1988.

Groome. Thomas. *Education for Life: A Spiritual Vision for Every Teacher and Parent*. Allen, Texas: Thomas More Press, 1998.

Hanh, Thich Nhat. *Peace Is Every Step: The Path of Mindfulness in Everyday Life*. New York: Bantam Books, 1991.

Hare, William. *What Makes a Good Teacher*. London, Ontario: The Althouse Press, 1993.

Haring, Bernard. *Free and Faithful in Christ: Moral Theology for Clergy and Laity*. New York, NY: Crossroad Books, 1978.

Harris, Maria. *Teaching and Religious Imagination: An Essay in the Theology of Teaching*. New York, NY: Harper Collins Publishers, 1991.

Holland, Joe. "Toward a Global Culture of Life: Cultural Challenges to Catholic Social Thought in the Postmodern Electronic-Ecological Era" in *Globalization and Catholic Social Thought: Present Crisis, Future Hope*. Eds. John A. Coleman and William F. Ryan. Maryknoll, NY: Orbis Books, 2005.

Ibish, Yusuf. *Traditional Modes of Contemplation and Action: A Colloquium held at Rothko Chapel Houston Texas*. London: Billings and Sons, Ltd., 1977.

Jacobs, Jane. *Dark Age Ahead*. Toronto: Vintage Canada, 2005.

Johnson, Robert A. *Owning Your Shadow: Understanding the Dark Side of the Psyche*. New York, NY: HarperCollins Publishers, 1993.

Jung, Carl. *The Portable Jung*. New York, NY: Penguin Books, 1971.

_____. *The Development of Personality: Papers on Child Psychology, Education, and Related Subjects*. New York, NY: Princeton University Press, 1981.

Leddy, Mary Jo. *Radical Gratitude*. Maryknoll, NY: Orbis Press, 2002.

Leddy, Mary Jo and Mary Ann Hinsdale, eds. *Faith That Transforms: Essays in Honor of Gregory Baum*. Mahweh, New Jersey: Paulist Press, 1987.

Lichtmann, Maria. *The Teacher's Way: Teaching and the Contemplative Life*. New York/ Mahwah, NJ: Paulist Press, 2005.

Lonergan, Bernard. *Collected Works of Bernard Lonergan: Topics in Education— The Cincinnati Lectures of 1959 on the Philosophy of Education*. Ed. Robert M. Doran. Toronto: University of Toronto Press, 1993.

_____. *Method in Theology*. New York: The Seabury Press, 1972.

McGowan, Mark G. *The Enduring Gift: Catholic Education in the Province of Ontario*. Toronto: Ontario Catholic School Trustees Association, 2001.

Merton, Thomas. *New Seeds of Contemplation*. London: Burns and Oates, 1967.

Miller, John P. *Educating for Wisdom and Compassion: Creating Conditions for Timeless Learning*. Thousand Oaks, California: Corwin Press, 2006.

_____. *Education and the Soul: Toward a Spiritual Curriculum*. Albany, NY: State University of New York Press, 2000.

_____. *The Contemplative Practitioner: Meditation in Education and the Professions.* Toronto: OISE Press, 1994.

_____. *The Holistic Teacher.* Toronto: OISE Press, 1993.

Miller, John P, et. al., eds. *Holistic Learning and Spirituality in Education: Breaking New Ground.* New York, NY: State University of New York Press, 2005.

Mitchell, Donald W. and James A. Wiseman, O.S.B. *The Gethsemani Encounter: A Dialogue on the Spiritual Life of Buddhist and Christian Monks.* New York: The Continuum Publishing Company, 1999.

Moore, Thomas. *Care of the Soul: A Guide for Cultivating Depth and Sacredness in Everyday Life.* New York, NY: Harper Perennial, 1992.

Noddings, Nel. *The Challenge to Care in Schools: An Alternative Approach to Education.* New York, NY: Teacher College Press, 1992.

O'Donoghue, John. *Anam Cara: A Book of Celtic Wisdom.* New York: HarperCollins, 1997.

Oliver, Donald W. *Education, Modernity, and Fractured Meaning: Toward a Process Theory of Teaching and Learning.* New York, NY: State University of New York Press, 1989.

O Murchu, Diarmuid. *Quantum Theology: Spiritual Implications of the New Physics.* New York, NY: Crossroad Publishing Company, 1998.

_____. *Reclaiming Spirituality.* New York: Crossroad Publishing Company, 1998.

O'Sullivan, Edmund. *Transformative Learning: Educational Vision for the 21st Century.* Toronto: University of Toronto Press, 1999.

Palmer, Parker. *The Active Life: Wisdom for Work, Creativity, and Caring.* San Francisco: HarperCollins, 1990.

_____. *The Courage to Teach: Exploring the Inner Landscape of a Teacher's Life.* San Francisco: Jossey-Bass Publishers, 1998.

_____. "The Grace of Great Things: Reclaiming the Sacred in Knowing, Teaching, and Learning" in *Holistic Education Review*, Vol. 10, No. 3, Fall 1997.

_____. *To Know As We Are Known: A Spirituality of Education.* San Francisco: Harper and Row, Publishers, 1983.

Panikkar, Raimundo. "The Contemplative Mood: A Challenge to Modernity" in *Cross Currents: The Wisdom of the Heart and the Life of the Mind.* Vol. 31, No. 3, Fall 1981.

_____. "The Dawn of Christianness" in *Cross Currents: The Wisdom of the Heart and the Life of the Mind.* Fiftieth Anniversary Issue, Vol. 50, Nos. 1–2, Spring/Summer 2000.

Plunkett, Dudley. *Secular and Spiritual Values: Grounds for Hope in Education.* London: Routledge, 1990.

Postman, Neil. *The End of Education: Redefining the Value of School.* New York, NY: Vintage Books, 1996.

Rawls, John. *A Theory of Justice.* Cambridge: Harvard University Press, 1971.

Ricoeur, Paul. *Lectures on Ideology and Utopia.* Ed. George H. Taylor. New York, NY: Columbia University Press, 1986.

_____. *Oneself as Another.* Trans. Kathleen Blamey. Chicago: University of Chicago Press, 1992.

Rolheiser, Ronald, author and editor. *Secularity and the Gospel: Being Missionaries to our Children.* New York: The Crossroad Publishing Company, 2006.

Russell, Kenneth C. "How Contemplatives Read the World" in *Spiritual Life: A Quarterly of Contemporary Spirituality.* Vol. 33, No. 4, Winter 1987.

Sardello, Robert. *Facing the World with Soul.* Hudson, NY: Lindisfarne Press, 1992.

Saul, John Ralston. *A Fair Country: Telling Truths About Canada.* Toronto: Viking Canada, 2008.

Sen, Amartya. *The Idea of Justice.* Cambridge, MA: The Belknap Press of Harvard University Press, 2009.

Shannon, William H. *Thomas Merton's Dark Path: The Inner Experience of a Contemplative.* New York, NY: Farrar, Straus, Giroux, 1981.

Sharp, Daryl. *Jung Lexicon: A Primer of Terms and Concepts.* Toronto: Inner City Books, 1991.

Suzuki, David. *The Sacred Balance: Rediscovering Our Place In Nature.* Vancouver, BC: Greystone Books, 1997.

Sweet, Lois. *God in the Classroom: The Controversial Issue of Religion in Canada's Schools.* Toronto: McClelland & Stewart, 1997.

Taylor, Charles. *A Secular Age.* Cambridge, Massachusetts: Harvard University Press, 2007.

_____. *The Malaise of Modernity.* Toronto: Anansi Press, 1991.

Ulanov, Ann and Barry Ulanov. *Primary Speech: A Psychology of Prayer.* Atlanta, Georgia: John Knox Press. 1982.

Vanier, Jean. *Becoming Human.* Toronto: Anansi Press, 1998.

Index

CPSIA information can be obtained at www.ICGtesting.com
Printed in the USA
269244BV00001B/6/P

9 780761 855538